Snapchat

How to Start on Snapchat for the Absolute

(Comprehensive Beginner's Guide to Learn Snapchat Marketing)

Roger Pressnell

Published By **Bella Frost**

Roger Pressnell

Snapchat: How to Start on Snapchat for the Absolute (Comprehensive Beginner's Guide to Learn Snapchat Marketing)

ISBN   978-0-9949175-8-4

No part of this guidebook shall be reproduced in any form without permission in writing from the publisher except in the case of brief quotations embodied in critical articles or reviews.

Legal & Disclaimer

Table Of Contents

Chapter 1: Getting Started With Snapchat

In this chapter, allow us to check all the basics of Snapchat and the way you can get commenced with this app.

What is Snapchat?

In the 3 hundred and sixty five days 2011, Snapchat modified into released. This became a social media software program or an app. The important motive of this app became to assist people to percentage pix in addition to films that would mechanically self-destruct interior seconds of the receiver receiving it and establishing it.

This is the feature that devices Snapchat apart at the same time as as compared to one among a type social media apps. It facilitates in preserving privateness. Ever because it come to be launched, Snapchat has turn out to be extremely famous and in recent times, it is considered to be one of the maximum extensively used social media programs. Snapchat is available for all mobile systems and this app become created genuinely so people need to express themselves in a better manner.

Celebrities, socialites, well-known personalities, nearly all and sundry has joined Snapchat and this honestly offers to its enchantment. Snapchat isn't extremely good easy to download, however it is also easy to apply.

When have become it released?

Snapchat have become released within the 12 months 2011, and it's been up to date more than one instances thinking about the truth that then. The gift model is famous and has been designed to inform the picks of a first rate amount of customers.

As consistent with the statistics available, there are extra than seven hundred million snaps which may be shared on a each day basis on Snapchat. This method that there are more than 900 snaps being shared on commonplace in step with second. These facts display the popularity of Snapchat. Snapchat is appeared as one of the fine apps for sending and receiving photographs.

Facebook had made a suggestion to Snapchat for amalgamation; but, this provide changed into declined thru its creators due to the truth they didn't need to leap on board the economic car. Facebook then attempted to release an app alongside the strains of Snapchat, called Slingshot. However, Slingshot did now not in form up to the popularity of Snapchat.

What is its reason?

In nowadays's international, wherein each person desires to percent pictures and motion pix, an app that is solely dedicated to this motive is, in reality, a high-quality preference. However, privacy issues have turn out to be a first-rate worry for people nowadays mainly whilst they may be sharing their images with others.

This is one hassle that Snapchat has efficaciously capitalized on. It turn out to be created with an aim of assisting human beings send or percentage their pix with others anywhere sooner or later of the globe, at the same time as no longer having to worry approximately the privacy risks. The snap shots will self-destruct interior some seconds and this doesn't deliver the receiver a hazard to shop them.

This characteristic is the maximum important selling component of this app!

Who can use Snapchat?

Originally, the audiences that Snapchat catered for have been teens and young adults. This app has functions much like the addition of filters that can be made use of for enhancing or enhancing the photo fantastic.

This function have end up right away popular with college college students and workplace goers. However, with the passage of time, even agencies started to appearance the potential of Snapchat for promoting their products and services. They started the use of it for selling their items to purchasers. They additionally began out to utilize this app for growing the recognition of their brand.

Many organizations now hire Snapchat for increasing their patron base and moreover for developing their earnings. You can start gaining the equal advantages via reading the only-of-a-type pointers and pointers which have been cited on this e-book.

How does Snapchat paintings?

At gift, Snapchat is taken into consideration to be amongst one of the tremendous apps which can be to be had for keeping in touch with friends and family. This is a easy software program application that permits its clients to share pics and films with brilliant ease. Snapchat moreover gives a platform for humans to talk with, or message, every one-of-a-kind.

This makes it fairly easy for human beings to preserve in contact with each exclusive and additionally for sharing photos and films with every other. The buddies and lovers of a consumer may be capable of take a look at the pix and movement photographs that the patron has shared and they are able to percentage their own with their fanatics as properly.

Getting began with Snapchat

It is in reality smooth to get started out with Snapchat. Here are the stairs for getting began out with it.

Step 1: The first step is to down load this app from the app keep. This utility is available on Android, iOS, and domestic home home windows app shops. Once the app has been downloaded, you will want to open it on your smartphone.

Step 2: Once you've got opened it, the app will ask you to fill in sure records like your e-mail cope with, a password, and your birthday. These facts are obligatory and you could want to go into them. The minimal age restrict for the usage of this utility is 13 years. If you aren't 13, then you may be redirected to an alternative app referred to as Snapkidz.

Step 3: The app will then maintain to confirm your identity by asking you a few questions. These are quite smooth and are normally visible questions.

Step 4: The next step can be to characteristic your contacts in your list. Snapchat will ask you to furnish get right of entry to to your contact listing. By doing so, you are robotically transferring all of your contacts on your Snapchat. However, if you aren't keen on doing so, then you could adjust the pal list and continue to feature best the ones individuals who you may want to have to your listing.

Step five: The next step could be to select your non-public possibilities. There is an possibility to be had for dealing with the filters, digital camera flash, reply tab, texts and so forth. You moreover have the selection of selecting human beings with whom you'll need to deliver and gain snaps.

Step 6: The next step is probably to make use of your cellphone's digital camera for taking snaps. These snaps may be shared with incredible human beings. The app has were given automatic access to the digicam and it allows you to take snap shots. You have the choice of which includes a tagline or a brief caption for personalizing the picture. There are wonderful filters that you may choose out from and people filters will help in improving the attraction of the pix taken.

Step 7: The subsequent step may be to ship the snap to a person with whom you may want to percentage it. Select the humans with whom you'll need to share the snap out of your friend listing and send it.

Step 8: You may be capable of attain snaps as nicely. You will truly need to visit obtained snaps for locating the pictures which you were despatched.

Step 9: Snapchat has additionally have been given the choice of collectively with a story. A tale could be a video or maybe a picture that might permit your fanatics recognize what you have got had been given been doing. A story lasts for twenty-4 hours and it self-destructs similar to the snaps after the expiration of the agreed time period.

Step 10: You have the choice of even beginning a chat consultation with a chum. This function is much like that of every other chat messengers available. The messages will seem one above the opposite. However, not like the other messengers, you acquired't be allowed to have a have a look at the previous chats once you shut up the window.

Myths Surrounding Snapchat

Snapchat is for humans, not businesses

This is a totally not unusual misconception that surrounds Snapchat. People remember that Snapchat is only designed for human beings and will not hold pinnacle for organizations. However, that is best a fable as it's far high-quality for businesses to promote their products and services. Companies will find out it handy to offer you with techniques the usage of photos and movies to achieve out to an audience.

Through the course of this e-book, we're capable of test the severa methods wherein you can use Snapchat for commercial enterprise employer talents.

Snapchat is overshadowed through other structures

This is some different misconception doing the rounds. People take delivery of as authentic with that Snapchat isn't as well-known as Facebook or Twitter. However, that is a incorrect evaluation as they're not all the same. Facebook and Twitter are exceptional from Snapchat in that they're used to promote messages.

Snapchat, however, is completely for picture promotions. This works better as humans may be interested by pix as compared to just text. Snapchat is in a league of its very private and now not suffering from competition from one-of-a-kind internet web websites.

Snapchat does now not allow advertising

Snapchat has a function called storytelling wherein humans can add in a series of snap shots to tell a tale. This characteristic is brilliant as groups can publish a series of snap shots about a marketing marketing campaign or maybe their products. This lets in them to market their products correctly.

It is a incredible tool to use to deliver throughout a message to the aim market, as they may have the potential to narrate to it higher. In fact, many businesses, large and small, now use Snapchat stories as a method to advertising advertising campaign their merchandise.

It will take time to installation oneself

This will rely on the sort of campaigns which can be being used. If the campaigns are exciting and you control to achieve quite a few enthusiasts then you'll installation yourself quite brief. You ought to make certain that you keep your content material up to date and offer your audiences with thrilling fabric. Only then will you be able to capitalize on Snapchat's fulfillment as a promotional device.

Snapchat stays in particular new to the sector of organization vending and does now not sell it as aggressively as Facebook and Twitter so it'll take a hint time on the manner to apply Snapchat to promote agency.

I am on Instagram so I don't need Snapchat

Instagram and Snapchat are not the identical. In truth, they're pretty severa and do now not war on any degree. Snapchat affords you with a platform in which pics are routinely destroyed after a positive aspect of time. This makes it great for lots kinds of agencies and allows them to give you new campaigns every so often.

The capabilities provided on Snapchat are also pretty extraordinary from the ones on Instagram. Therefore, in case you need a outstanding platform to sell your business enterprise then Snapchat is the best for you.

Chapter 2: Snapchat- Future of Social Media

Social media structures like Facebook, Twitter, and LinkedIn despite the fact that have a robust maintain on the area of social media because of the sheer type of clients. There are a handful of various social media apps and systems which may be in search of to create a place for themselves. Snapchat takes region to be among those and it has the most powerful capacity too.

It now not only has the potential for building a customer base that could rival the essential channels stated above, however it is also growing enough have an effect at the manner wherein other structures are growing. Let us check the reasons why Snapchat has this form of well capability.

Younger demographic

Statistics recorded via Snapchat display that above seventy one% in their customers are underneath the age of 35. There are 3 vital motives why it's miles believed that the more youthful generations are answerable for the usage of the present day tendencies. The first motive is they hold a extraordinary chew of the buying strength and this has a tendency to attract most of the corporations and agencies who use it.

The second reason is that they are the maximum adaptable of the lot and can without trouble adapt to new systems. The zero.33 and the essential purpose is that there is a opportunity that they'll decide upon the structures they elderly with and will deliver the identical into the mainstream.

Privacy

One of the number one motives for the increase and fulfillment of Snapchat is the way in which it treats consumer content material cloth. The snaps are automatically deleted completely after a fixed time frame. This allows in ensuring man or woman privacy. There had been main protection and statistics breaches in maximum vital agencies; clients are skeptical about what they're inclined to percentage. Platforms that could come to be privy to such threats and address the ones will expand over the subsequent couple of years.

Innovation

Snapchat maintains on such as new features and skills. There is not any sign that it'll sluggish down each time quickly. The new skills that Snapchat keeps on such as aren't drawn from those of its competition. These abilties haven't been mimicked or mainstream.

Dominance

Mobile devices are becoming mainly well-known and their popularity is growing via the day. Most of the well-known structures have a computer and cellular utility like Facebook and Twitter. Snapchat has advanced an app this is mainly designed for mobile phones. They have introduced one in every of a kind abilities to enhance functionality like vertical movies. Snapchat is making an attempt to make the most of the medium for which it changed into superior.

Learning curve

The reading curve this is crucial for using the app is considered one of its maximum counterintuitive abilties. It is easy to begin using Snapchat; however, it's going to take some time earlier than you have enough revel in for making the outstanding use of this platform. It not extremely good encourages new clients but it moreover rewards prolonged-term use. This permits it to create a notable analyzing curve that allows in maintaining clients.

Immediate posts

Immediate placed up or within the 2d posts are pretty famous now. Snapchat and Instagram cater to this craze. Even social media giants like Facebook have end up this on board thru functions like Facebook Live.

Chapter 3: Connecting With Your Snapchat Followers

Most of the manufacturers and companies tend to allocate time and energy for growing content with a purpose to assist them in enticing their clients. In this financial disaster, allow us to test the one of a kind strategies wherein businesses and brands can hook up with their fans on Snapchat.

Finding your creative aspect

Snapchat is clearly beneficial for organizations that have have been given a message to share. It isn't only for groups that are looking to boom the patron traffic to their internet internet web site or for developing downloads.

If you consider you studied that there's a story behind your emblem, then Snapchat will certainly are to be had available. You may be capable of create a foothold for your self via way of showcasing your brand in a one of a kind mild. It might be through progressive storytelling, celeb meet-ups, concert events or perhaps adventures.

Make high-quality that you are telling the story of your emblem thru posting content material material material from such an environment or surroundings that would constitute it.

Do not over market it

It is specially easy to sincerely swipe down or maybe faucet via the testimonies on Snapchat. Therefore, the tale which you are posting have to be such that it could without problems take keep of the viewer's attention and it ought to be speedy paced. The goal market shouldn't lose interest. If you want to make accurate use of Snapchat, then keep utilizing the added filters and emojis.

Get as modern as viable. Make the store seem "cool" and make visitors keen for more. You will want to keep posting particular content fabric on a every day basis and you may want to have interaction as well as assemble your target market by including thrilling content material material for you to get your message inside the course of.

Spokesperson

It is specifically vital that you find out the "proper" spokesperson for representing your brand. It is important that you may tie up with someone who has were given an goal market and moreover is aware of a way to make the most of this app.

There are quite some social media influencers starting from musicians and singers to actors. Just having a large target marketplace base is not critical, they will also want to comprehend the high-quality manner in which they could optimize the app and make the maximum of it. They will want on the way to interact the target market too. You wouldn't need to tie up with someone who is virtually seeking to document their data to their boss.

You will need someone who's aware about his or her way spherical this app. It might be an character or an organisation and expertise the content fabric and the way in which it's far published are essential.

Increasing customer engagement

Audience engagement may be accelerated through manner of posting memories or a group of films or photographs on Snapchat that can be replayed for a duration of 24 hours. However, with the advent of the present day function that allows in replying to a specific snap or a video thru swiping the lowest of the show and by way of organising a ultra-modern chat the app is extra interactive.

This way that the entrepreneurs will now be able to collect remarks for the snaps that they may be posting. This is a superb way wherein you may be able to see in case your advertising and marketing campaign is working or not. You can snap another time your target market, open their snaps, encompass them to your story, and supply them freebies too. This will preserve them engaged and they'll be excited via what they will be doing too.

Chapter 4: What the Snapchat Terms Mean

Snapchat without a doubt has were given its very personal jargon. When you're aware about this, you may be in a position to talk more clearly.

Snaps

This refers back to the individual pix which might be sent and purchased in Snapchat. Snaps are shared together together with your pals and family members. The equal snap can be despatched throughout to multiple Snapchatters. All those who employ Snapchat are referred to as the Snapchatters. These snaps don't ultimate for added than ten seconds in advance than they self-destruct. You can without a doubt have the choice of choosing the time for which a snap could be to be had for viewing.

Snapback

This is the term that is used while a respond is given to a specific snap. To located it surely, it's miles the reaction that you would likely have acquired from the other Snapchatters for the snap that you despatched them. You can also degree the sort of snapbacks that you have given and those who've acquired it as properly.

Story

A story is probably a set of snap shots or possibly snaps that may be added one after the other to the account. These can then be regarded with the aid of the usage of your fans as commonly as they would really like to. However, a story might be available for only 24 hours. Each tale may be a story of a specific event which you were part of or any interest in which you participated. You also can view the memories posted by means of your buddies within the tale phase discovered to your account.

Scores

There are facts which might be supplied to a selected man or woman primarily based at the amount of snaps received, despatched, snapbacks and so on. All those diverse matters are taken underneath consideration for offering the rating of an person. You also have the choice of viewing your buddy's score as well to recognize the quantity of snaps that haven't been despatched or received.

Snapcode

Snapcodes are a in reality smooth manner for inclusive of new buddies on your account. You can hire your mobile phone for scanning and along with new pals or clients for your account. It isn't handiest clean, however it's miles short as properly. You can get proper of get right of entry to in your Snapcode with the aid of tapping on the ghost icon which you study on your mobile cellphone.

Snapstreak

This refers back to the consecutive variety of days for that you have been sharing your snaps at the side of your pal on Snapchat. It is particularly crucial which you maintain sharing as many photographs as viable. This is the number one characteristic of this app.

Friends and Followers

There is a large difference between buddies and fans in your Snapchat account. The humans who have been brought from your contact listing are called pals. You get the choice of inclusive of friends for your pal list through clicking at the plus image that looks on the right hand corner of the web page.

Followers are the human beings who have started out following you, however you aren't following them. These names will show up to your account as a listing of fans.

Lenses

This refers to the superb modifications that you may rent for the images taken. These are real-time consequences that may be without problem brought onto your snaps. There are particular filters that you can pick out from and each of those is precise. These lenses are free and they'll be made use of for reinforcing your pics. These topics exchange frequently and you will no longer get bored with these.

Filters

Filters are the overlays that may be delivered onto your pictures. These are supposed to make your snap shots appear extra interesting. There are one in every of a type filters that you could select out from and every of those offers a exceptional impact. The filters are notably famous thinking about the truth that they permit you to vicinity a laugh photos about the area in your pictures.

There are certain popular acronyms which you must understand for consolation sake. FTFY approach regular that for you. If you've got were given had been given consistent some thing for someone and want to make an apology for the same then you could make use of FTFY. This can also be made use of for boosting a photo. HIFW stands for a manner I felt while.

This signifies a feeling that you have expert. This is normally used for signifying a funny scenario. JSYK stands for in fact so you apprehend; it is also used as an opportunity for FYI. TIL stands for these days, I placed and SMH stands for shaking my head. These are some of the acronyms which may be usually used.

Chapter 5: Building Your Brand Using Snapchat

Wondering how you may employ Snapchat to your business? Do you need to create a deeper bond along with your Snapchat lovers? In this economic catastrophe, you may study the most effective-of-a-type techniques in which you could employ Snapchat for your commercial enterprise corporation.

Staging an influencer display screen

McDonald's is a worldwide fast meals large and that they aren't only for the redheaded clown and their meals with toys. Before launching their new bacon clubhouse sandwich, more than one professional athletes like LeBron James gave all of the clients a 'behind the curtain' appearance. They partnered with athletes for selling their product. McDonald's did no longer percentage the results of this promotional hobby.

It is steady to assume that it went well for the motive that it went on for pretty some time. Their promotion changed into pushed to particular social media like Twitter, in which the clients were asked to comply with once more. McDonald's has over 3 million fanatics on their Twitter contend with. The equal philosophy that McDonald's made use of can be applied to any organization. Give your customers a sneak peek of ways subjects get finished.

Even if your advertising and advertising and marketing and advertising and marketing finances takes vicinity to be a small fraction of the McDonald's one, the consumers will still be interested in reading what's taking place.

Supporting an account takeover

If you need your message to be visible, then you could allow an influential Snapchatter to take over your patron account. You may not have connections with loads of heaps of followers. However, even being capable of rope in a close-by authority may be of wonderful help.

For instance, a apparel save Wet Seal released a Snapchat marketing marketing campaign and the same have grow to be taken over with the aid of MsMeghanMakeup, a Snapchatter who has over 3 hundred,000 fans. Her affect helped the advertising marketing campaign.

Sharing your promo codes

You can offer your Snapchat followers with Snapchat exquisite coupons or promo codes for boosting your brand visibility. For example, the frozen yogurt chain- 16 made use in their Snapchat lovers and the without delay image characteristic for promoting their brand. They were moreover among the primary logo that made use of the coupon gives on Snapchat. The yogurt agency received new clients with the resource of selling superb particular places of their shops at a specific time.

People ought to need to get there and snap photos of themselves or their buddies consuming the frozen yogurt from sixteen Handles. They ought to straight away gather a reduction code for a discount from 16% to a hundred%. However, there's a trap. This might be legitimate for ten seconds.

Giving VIP access

It took severa weeks earlier than the images from New York Fashion week ought to trickle all of the manner right down to the purchasers. However, with Snapchat, enthusiasts may be supplied with on the spot updates. Snapchat can be made use of for sharing right now updates from any essential activities.

The editor in chief of Lucky Magazine had shared the snaps of various fashions even as strutting at the runway. This revolutionized the way in which people received the present day facts and snap shots from iconic sports in real time. Your lovers may be able to see the court instances from any event in case you deliver them a VIP get right of entry to to it on Snapchat.

Featuring your followers

Make effective that your Snapchat feed isn't continuously about yourself. Include your enthusiasts in it and you could furthermore incorporate them in the technique of content creation. The on line food ordering issuer GrubHub released their first advertising and marketing and advertising advertising marketing campaign on Snapchat in 2013.

They used to feature their weekly content and could embody content material fabric accrued from customers, any giveaways, and promotions as nicely. This projected a 20% increase of their style of fans.

Providing a demo

The on line retailing huge Amazon made use of Snapchat for now not best giving a demo about their voice-activated speaker Echo, but additionally made use of it promotional features as well. This helped in presenting some clarity to the forced customers whilst Echo changed into released.

It managed to accumulate more than 6100 mentions in an awful lot a great deal much less than 4 hours. If your emblem has lately launched a modern technology or a product, then you can appoint Snapchat for presenting a virtual guide to the manner in which the product is for use.

Partnering with influencers

You can add some well-known Snapchatters and then get them to conform with you too. This will surely help in growing your follower base and their fanatics will take to you as properly. Search for some of the famous ones to your location and begin following them.

You can also electronic mail them and then add your Snapchat code within the e-mail or your name at the way to be easy for them to examine you.

Addressing any relevant issue

Don't be afraid to be actual even as the use of this media. For example, the advertising campaign run by means of the usage of Dove is an instance of this. The cleaning cleaning soap logo Dove appealed to the older phase of the society until it reached out to the more youthful lot by using Snapchat. Over hours, 30 women were given to talk with psychologists and extraordinary ambassadors of this logo on Snapchat and that they have been given to percentage their mind and mind approximately the issues on vanity. These hints had been considered through Dove.

Post every day

It is rather important that you hold posting on a each day foundation and that you preserve your audiences often up to date. This is the only manner in which you could keep them coming decrease returned for more and pique their hobby.

Think of various matters that you may do to seize their interest. You can keep track of what one-of-a-kind agencies do and try and in form up. It obtained't be clean. However, as quickly as you've got controlled to get the hold of it, then you can actually see a great alternate in your commercial enterprise employer.

Public reminiscences

Make fine that all the recollections which you are posting are public. This is surprisingly critical seeing that humans will want to go through what you're sharing with them.

The testimonies will robotically destruct themselves after 24 hours after which you'll need to characteristic a cutting-edge one. However, in case you want to preserve exclusivity thru sharing fantastic matters that only a few customers can view, then you definately have that choice available too. This will clearly assist in making them revel in specific and enhance your emblem name.

Other systems

It is a fantastic concept to link all your social media payments. This might consist of your profiles on Twitter, Facebook, and LinkedIn too. It becomes an awful lot much less complicated to percentage records and make the content material fabric extra relatable to your fanatics. Continuing the identical marketing campaign sooner or later of specific systems will make sure that there may be some uniformity and it's going to help in connecting higher with the target market.

Expand contacts

Snapchat accesses your contact listing and permits in such as pals. It will assist you in developing your contact listing and thereby growth your reach. Make use of these leads and ship messages on your buddies. They may be capable of see any updates published by means of manner of you and realize the content fabric material that they may be being provided.

You shouldn't allow skip of a unmarried opportunity that will help you in reigning in a capacity purchaser. Tap into the friend lists of your buddies and pals for developing your following.

Groups

You have to make sure that you are a part of appropriate businesses on numerous terrific social media networks. This will assist you in staying in touch with others who can be useful on your business enterprise. There are severa forums available on-line in which you can leave your Snapchat name for others to add you. You can begin citing any concern rely which you need and begin a communicate on those groups.

Variety

The photos and memories you put up shouldn't be predictable. Post matters with a purpose to marvel and excite your goal market. You will want to function rate to the content cloth cloth that you are posting. If they discover comparable content material fabric material a few area else, it'd defeat the motive. Keep subjects exciting and unique on your goal marketplace.

Up up to now

Make certain that the content and the fabric which you are using to your snaps is updated. They want to function the ultra-current filters and lenses. Making use of the antique and redundant capabilities will truely make it stupid on your goal market. Posting viral content material material will help with numbers too.

Chapter 6: Metrics to Monitor When Using Snapchat

Snapchat is a remarkable platform that need to be explored thru marketers and it is so for an splendid reason. There are more than 6 billion each day video perspectives that have been delivered through Snapchat on a every day foundation. That's a huge quantity. Facebook has about eight million each day video views and YouTube spherical four billion.

What is one-of-a-kind about Snapchat is that each one those views are from mobile devices completely. This is a big opportunity for entrepreneurs and a platform available for brands to inform their testimonies. About 3-quarters of the customers within the US are over 18 years and increasingly clients belonging to the 20's have become a member of Snapchat too.

There are many entrepreneurs who've been spending time to without a doubt get used to this platform, however there may be one factor that is though tough human beings. This is the manner in which achievement of unique content material cloth fabric may be measured on Snapchat.

Marketers preserve struggling to make sense of the facts this is available to them. It is genuinely comprehensible why they wouldn't understand how to analyze facts on a new platform like Snapchat without any formal analytics.

Marketers shouldn't interest lots on the fans they have got and need to as a substitute attention at the style of those who are lapping up the reminiscences posted. Let us take a look at the maximum essential metrics that you will need to display display while the usage of Snapchat.

Total Unique Views

The fashionable unique views stands for the sort of humans who have opened the number one body within the Snapchat story you published at some stage in at the least one

2d. This can be completed with the aid of taking a take a look at the quantity of people who have opened the primary snap of your story inside the 24-hour time frame.

Users are allowed to submit as many snaps as they want and every snap can't be extra than 10 seconds prolonged. Users get to take a look at a snap story in some unspecified time in the future of the 24 hours for which it is available. One clearly exciting detail approximately the Total Unique Views metrics is on par with what Snapchat provides.

If you've got got paid Snapchat for on foot advertisements in your platform, then you definitely definately definately have paid for on foot a 10-2d video within the story. You can create as many ten-second movies as you need to. This approach that the man or woman advertisements that you can create will help in handing over greater content material fabric fabric and attractive your goal marketplace more than a ten-2d advert.

Total Story Completions

A tale on Snapchat can be virtually one snap or maybe a hundred snaps. The quality storytellers employ the 24-hour time body to be had on Snapchat for stringing collectively more than one snaps for growing a single video. When you have got published one single tale that has more than one frames, then you may need to test the type of humans who have taken into consideration the final snap. This will assist in measuring the huge type of human beings who've surely watched the entire video and feature fed on the story.

Completion Rate

A Snapchat is quite just like a storybook. It has an creation, then there's a story, and an forestall to that story as nicely. Thankfully, Snapchat permits its customers to peer the shape of humans who have taken into consideration each economic spoil. The of completion price is the part of humans who have started viewing the tale in comparison to the amount of those who considered the finishing of the story.

Facebook and YouTube will be inclined to suppose final touch charge as a way to degree engagement. The target market on Snapchat has a tendency to view the entire content material at one bypass regardless of the reality that the manufacturers hold on posting all day prolonged.

Screenshots

On Snapchat, in comparison to exclusive social media structures, there's no opportunity for liking, commenting, or sharing something. However, customers have the selection of checking the amount the human beings who have taken the screenshots in their snaps. This can be made use of as a device for engagement as properly.

For example, you may additionally encourage people to screenshot their selections in a "pick your non-public adventure" sort of a story. Alternatively, you can moreover rent screenshots as a technique of polling. You can ask humans to screenshot their personal favored a number of the product designs available for gathering their feedback. You can record the sizeable variety of screenshots of unique topics and then follow up along side your clients.

Chapter 7: Advantages of Using Snapchat

The amazing photo-sharing app this is presently to be had is Snapchat. In this financial ruin, allow us to test the splendid benefits that are available for the use of Snapchat.

Point of view

The biggest benefit of using Snapchat is that it lets in in acquiring a firsthand attitude of a person's world. Friends and family will be capable of see topics inside the identical manner in which you are seeing them.

This will help in sharing of extra information. Your goal market may be able to see topics the manner you spot them. They may be able to see it at the same time which you are seeing it and this makes it extra particular.

Timing

The tales posted on Snapchat simplest final for twenty-four hours and this make it fairly easy and to be had for humans. It is perfect for people who do no longer like retaining too many snap shots or movies. Their snaps will disappear as soon as the precise time is up.

This is a great manner in which you could keep your privacy and but preserve in touch collectively collectively along with your target audience. The pics won't be available lengthy sufficient for someone to misuse it. Even if a person takes a screenshot of a few element you despatched and you could get a notification if this takes region.

Buzz

This is a extraordinary platform for developing buzz about some issue. The app will permit you to create quick films that can be used as a teaser for a few component. You can create a quick preview for developing a buzz approximately an event amongst your fanatics.

This works without a doubt properly for all individuals who need to sell themselves or their companies. You ought to make viral movies and effects bring together an audience.

Ease

It is simply easy to make use of Snapchat. As you may have collected with the aid of the usage of now, that is one of the most person-first-class apps which can be available inside the marketplace at present. It can be used for chatting and sharing pics. The app is character-great and the man or woman interface is amusing to apply.

Snapchat for corporation

Snapchat is a clearly right manner in which you can beautify your industrial enterprise and beautify any industrial company possibilities which might be available for you. This is a splendid platform in case you want to cowl any live occasion. The goal marketplace can be concerned in the form of contests and live activities.

This will assist in maintaining your target market fascinated and additionally boom your goal market base. There are many businesses which might be using this platform for creating a buzz approximately their services and products. A small trailer or preview of what's in store for clients may be given and this could sincerely assist in capturing their hobby and thrilling your goal market.

The common age institution of clients consists of teens and goes as lots as 34 years. This way that it'd be clearly smooth to cause the younger target audience and hook up with them. This is also perhaps the most difficult age organisation to satisfaction. Snapchat makes it tons much less complex for manufacturers to reap out and connect to this target audience.

You can publish at the back of the scene pix and movies to make your goal market experience more related to the emblem. This is also a remarkable platform for assignment any giveaway. A giveaway will assist your customers experience more concerned and this will be the praise for their loyalty.

Snapchat is a first-rate manner to connect with them. You may have a examine extra approximately using Snapchat for marketing and advertising your organization or logo within the subsequent bankruptcy.

Chapter 8: Using Snapchat for Business

Snapchat is an exceedingly useful device for all groups and it helps within the retention of customers as well. It become certainly launched with the purpose of centered on young adults and teenagers. However, it quick have emerge as an exceptionally famous manner of selling services and products too. We took a study a number of the strategies in which Snapchat is beneficial for a business enterprise. Let us take a few greater blessings and the steps for installing region a Snapchat account for a commercial organization.

Snapchat is taken into consideration to be among the most used social networking media round the sector. There are more than a hundred million energetic customers registered on it and this makes it a clearly appropriate platform for selling organizations and brands on it. However, many agencies even though normally usually generally tend to pick out Facebook and Twitter for promoting themselves.

A have a take a look at indicates that great about 2% of the pinnacle businesses appoint Snapchat for advertising themselves. This shows that there can be a brilliant scope for advertising and marketing on right proper here for a organisation to take advantage of. Upcoming agencies can capitalize in this opportunity for the motive that they may not be part of the rat race with all of the special huge enterprise homes. This is likewise an extremely good opportunity for all the ones groups which may be nicely installation and are seeking out a cutting-edge manner in which they may growth their audience base.

Snapchat is providing them with a manner wherein they may be capable of increase their sales. A nicely-defined timeline is some different important advantage of using Snapchat. This manner that the target audience will no longer get compelled or distracted thru any muddle and all the snaps may additionally moreover have their important vicinity.

It is crucial to take into consideration that using Snapchat for the functions of enterprise may be excellent from making use of it as a social networking device for interacting along with your friends and family. You will need to adopt a unique technique in this situation. This interest need to take shipping of hobby due to the fact that people must realise that they may be interacting with a organization or a logo and now not simply an person.

That being said, it shouldn't be too intense or the target market will become bored. It is critical to symbolize the company within the notable viable way and offer a hazard for the target audience to connect with it. Here are the steps that you may be trying to observe for installing a Snapchat profile for your business enterprise.

Step 1: The first step might be to installation of the app. Follow the same instructions that have been stated in Chapter 1.

Step 2: While you are installing area your account, make sure that it is as expert as it can be. The name of your employer or company have to be the Snapchat call. This will allow people to apprehend that it is the reliable profile of the agency. The profile photo is probably the brand of your corporation. For example, Disney makes use of their real emblem to be positioned as their profile picture inside the center of the ghost. If your brand is not recognizable, then you may add the call of your agency to that.

Step 3: Now you will need to add your buddies. This will help in growing a right away base of target market and will make sure that you are starting up on the right foot. They might be able to see what you are posting after which give you with their remarks. Based on all this, you may make the crucial changes for your advertising and marketing marketing marketing campaign for making your content material material extra exciting.

Step 4: You will want to discover distinctive businesses and then begin following them. This will assist you in amassing statistics approximately what they will be into and the marketing techniques that they will be using. You will want to keep a song of the strategies made use of by way of the use of your business employer and also the things they will be posting. This will without a doubt bypass an extended way in supporting you come up with better promotional campaigns for your enterprise.

Step five: You will need to select and construct your own target audience base. This is a very crucial step of this approach. You will need to accumulate as many lovers as viable in case you want at the manner to attain out to a massive goal marketplace. This is similar to finding as many Twitter fanatics as feasible on Twitter.

Step 6: You can begin following a few well-known celebrities on Snapchat. Doing this could help you in enhancing your target market base. If you have were given were given any private contacts with such celebrities, then you could request them to add you to their buddy list for enhancing your visibility.

Step 7: You will need to start developing snaps and tales if you want to appeal on your target market. This will help you a extraordinary deal. After carrying out a certain component, then you may begin focusing on constructing a more potent connection with a smaller target market and gather particular techniques to definitely cater for them.

Step 8: Make tremendous that you have set a hard and speedy time for updating your snaps and memories. This will allow humans to apprehend even as they will be able to count on an replace and they may additionally get used to checking the snaps from your commercial employer at a particular time.

Chapter 9: Snapchat Marketing Strategies

Snapchat is a first-rate level which will marketplace the products and services supplied by means of the use of way of your brand or business agency. Here, we take a look at a few Snapchat strategies for boosting your organisation.

Contests

Organizing one among a kind contests for your Snapchat is certainly a exquisite concept. People may be in a position to take part in them and relate higher for your business enterprise. The contests can be whatever from deciding on a caption on your snap shots or setting up images with the product bought with the aid of your company.

All of those are great processes to sell your Snapchat account and marketplace products and services. The giveaway after the competition ends want to be precise or worth just so human beings located their high-quality try. Announce the opposition on all your special social media platforms earlier just so humans recognise when to participate in it.

Events

Announcing sports for your customers via Snapchat can be of help. The platform offers a amazing opportunity to convey your customers collectively. Post invites for them and ask them to screenshot it. Whoever has it may appear on the occasion. This makes for a extraordinary way to interact your target market and get them to RSVP to the event.

Again, announce it on all your social media structures genuinely so humans mentioned approximately it earlier. Ask them on the event whether or not or no longer they favored the concept and would love to have more of it. Plan your future campaigns based mostly on their reaction.

Tie-u.S.Nbsp;

It is a extremely good idea to tie up with distinct groups on Snapchat. Doing so will assist you change fans. For example, positioned up a picture and ask your fanatics to screenshot it. The same can artwork as a chit to get reduce charge for your accomplice's products and vice versa.

However, don't forget to tie up with businesses that have same or extra enthusiasts than you as as a manner to be honest exercise. Once you've got were given a thriving run you'll be able to tie up with others loads much less complicated. You want not limit it to simply one associate and tie up with as many as you want.

Offers

Provide specific reductions and special offers on your Snapchat best. This can be some element like coupon codes to advantage a reduction, buy one get one loose and so forth. These gives must be absolutely available on your Snapchat account on my own and not anywhere else. However, you may promote it approximately it to your different systems so as to inform your customers about the equal.

Try to vary the gives now and again an tremendous way to maintain the target marketplace engaged. Look at what some of the gives with the useful resource of rival corporations and in shape as a lot as it. Again, provide you with modern techniques to announce the gives for your Snapchat account.

Previews

Snapchat is a excellent location as a manner to provide a sneak-top into your upcoming services and products. Add a image or video of what is to come again and your audience may be on the threshold of their seats. Incorporate a game here additionally and make it exciting.

Ask them to take a screenshot of a particular product from the most current series that they'll be capable of win. Similarly, assume up distinctive strategies wherein to marketplace your merchandise the usage of Snapchat to acquire out to a larger purpose marketplace.

Media Exclusives

A incredible trick to growth fanatics is to offer unique merchandise thru Snapchat by myself. For example, great your fans on Snapchat may also have access to a specific series. These may be specific in terms of color, layout, or pattern. You will have to inform them without a doubt that they'll be definitely to be had via Snapchat by myself and no longer everywhere else. Consider introducing an entire exquisite line of products which is probably only available thru your Snapchat account.

Merchandize

Offer customers exceptional products. This merchandise will bring your business corporation's name and brand. You additionally have the selection to function their call or each other facts that they would like to have at the products. Customizing merchandise for customers permits them preserve coming yet again for added and Snapchat can play a thing in it.

Celebrities

Celebrities paintings like magic in phrases of garnering interest. Start following celebrities and get them to examine you. This will create a buzz approximately your company. Keep your first-rate buddy list open for people see, as they'll comprehend who's to your listing. The equal extends to having popular Snapchatters in your listing.

Others might be able to see who you've got were given were given and beautify your account's enchantment. There are many style models to comply with. It might be extraordinary if you can get honestly one among them to put on or use your products and use the identical for your account.

Rewards

Offer your customers rewards which includes incentives for following your Snapchat account. That will ensure you boom the extensive type of enthusiasts. The rewards can be bargain coupons or shop credit rating that the lovers can use to get reductions and precise gives. Announce the equal earlier and on top notch systems as nicely.

Referrals

Offer rewards for referrals as properly. This is a trick that many organizations now use to draw fans. Announce a reward for people who supply in extraordinary enthusiasts. The reward should be profitable sufficient to draw people and keep them involved.

Chapter 10: Leveraging Social Media for Making Money

Up till now, we had been looking on the unique approaches wherein social media can be made use of thru a commercial enterprise business enterprise. In this bankruptcy, allow us to test the strategies wherein an person can make use of social media for making more money.

Writing backed posts

There are many web web sites, corporations and types that could provide their lovers and their patron's possibilities for sharing backed posts for promoting the goods and services provided via the usage of them. This is a outstanding manner wherein you may earn cash by way of way of utilising social media. You needn't have any merchandise of your personal for sale.

The first step for purchasing commenced with subsidized posts is probably to grow your follower base on multiple social media systems collectively with Facebook, Twitter,

Instagram, or maybe Snapchat. You will need to have an awesome go with the glide of website traffic to your weblog if you need businesses to provide you money for writing about them. You will need to have more than 5000 internet net page perspectives each month to your weblog.

Once you've got got controlled to build up an incredible range of enthusiasts and readers, then you could start earning money via subsidized posts. It is critical that you have managed to strike a stability among the posts which you write and the subsidized posts. If you start sharing too many subsidized posts, then your readers will become bored and this isn't the tremendous manner ahead. You need to percent sponsored posts in a strategic manner and don't make the content material of the sponsored posts seem too bland or stupid.

Promoting partner products

Promoting accomplice products may additionally even assist you in being worthwhile. Make effective that you are selling excellent such products that you have used and such merchandise which you realise will assist your goal marketplace. If you are looking for methods in which you can begin selling accomplice merchandise or are seeking out companion merchandise, then you may need to start mastering.

You will need to search for groups whose merchandise you appoint and notice if they offer any companion possibilities. Focusing on the products that your target marketplace need and desires will assist you in becoming a achievement. Becoming an Amazon Associate may additionally even help you in earning earnings thru promoting products that you use. You can start selling such products on any of your social media profiles and percent them with their companion link.

In addition, writing up sincere reviews will help in attracting and preserving the bear in mind of your customers. Another manner in which you can sell accomplice products is thru developing a Resources web net page. This will assist you in giving a detailed listing of all of the topics that you make use of for walking your blog and the tremendous products which you promote.

Becoming a social media supervisor

Social media manipulate has end up a superb mission. Small and large companies alike are the usage of social media more than they ever did. This opens up jobs for individuals who are proper at coping with profiles in the course of one-of-a-type social media net websites. The best way to move about this will be to sign up for a career net web site after which look out for any hobby postings or any other freelancing jobs.

Promoting your very personal offerings

You can employ social media for promoting the services which you are imparting. Social media will help in connecting you with your best audience. You can promote your offerings quite with out problem with the aid of way of in conjunction with statistics approximately the identical into your weblog posts and so on.

Chapter 11: What Separates Snapchat from Other Social Media

Snapchat became launched within the twelve months 2011. However, its presence wasn't felt till the 365 days 2013. Facebook had attempted and miserably did now not snub it. Brands have been type of gradual in embracing this specific platform. Snapchat is a messaging app that allows the customers to supply snaps within the varieties of images or films so one can be mechanically destructed after being taken into consideration.

This platform is to be had for handiest smartphones. The sender has the option of selecting the quantity of time for which the snap may be considered after which the snap may be long gone all the time.

The one function that permits in making Snapchat particular from distinctive social media networks is that it has an functionality to shape a personal connection with the receiver. Unlike the opposite social networking internet websites wherein the posts are public, at the same time as a snap is brought it appears more tailored and personal.

A snap may be despatched to a whole institution, however even then, it has the customised contact to it. This offers the business enterprise an capacity to form a private bond with a person. Snaps acquired from someone else can't be forwarded. This ensures that the content material cloth cloth is glowing and precise. Snapchat stands apart from Facebook, Twitter, or a few other social media platform because it lets in the groups in interacting with their clients in a non-public and jovial manner.

The age corporations among 13 and 25 can't be resultseasily reached on well-known networking systems like Facebook or Twitter. Snapchat facilitates in attractive to a far more younger goal market and this can be made use of with the beneficial resource of producers for coming close to the target market they could in no way have reached in advance than.

The abilities supplied through Snapchat keep on growing. Snapchat allows the man or woman to create an remarkable narrative within the form of reminiscences. These tales could be snap shots or movies which have been strung collectively. This may be viewed a couple of times within the time frame of 24 hours. After this term is over, the clip might be routinely eliminated. Being able to build a tale does pass an extended way at the same time as you are attempting to have interaction your goal market.

This lets in in preserving your aim marketplace engaged all day prolonged. If you're willing within the path of using Snapchat on your advertising and advertising and advertising and marketing and advertising advertising campaign then you could want to keep its time restriction feature in view. The purpose Snapchat has obtained recognition is because of the time span that permits in grabbing viewer's hobby. All the protection breaches of facts have made Internet customers quite skeptical approximately the information this is shared on critical social networking systems.

When it includes Snapchat, it allows in constructing their confidence due to the fact the statistics that they'll be sharing will no longer be to be had after the expiration of the time restriction. You will no longer must type via loads of hundreds of messages on a platform like Snapchat.

Engaging a small target market is in fact essential for organizations. It is as crucial as garnering the attention of a larger target audience. It is not quite a great deal the range of fanatics that you have were given, it's also about the wide style of fans who care. The vast type of fans you've got controlled to engage together with your content subjects. The one to one enjoy that Snapchat lets in in growing is a super manner for undertaking higher costs of engagement. This perceived intimacy is pretty beneficial.

Chapter 12: Identifying a Target Audience

Before you could get began out with developing some exciting content material fabric, you could want to direct your interest towards finding and building your aim market. For constructing an purpose marketplace, you may need to determine your target. Snapchat doesn't cater to all audiences, it is a awesome advertising and advertising tool, however it can not paintings for all kinds of commercial enterprise corporation.

As mentioned in advance, Snapchat appeals to the younger demographic. If your goal marketplace is in the 13-26 age bracket, then you could hire it.

If you are new to Snapchat, then the earlier chapters have all the fundamental facts that you can require for purchasing started with it. It is ideal to realize how you can find people or tremendous agencies on Snapchat. However, you want to additionally be worried approximately making sure that human beings are able to discover your brand or company and are adding you as properly.

Building an audience for your self shouldn't be too difficult if you have controlled to create an lively and engaged audience for your self on numerous different social networking structures. If folks that are following you on one of a kind social media web sites are also gift on Snapchat, it is probable that they might have brought you.

The foundation is already completed and you will sincerely need to tell your lovers which you are on Snapchat and ask them to conform with you. You can positioned up information approximately the identical on diverse awesome social media payments of yours for alerting your fanatics.

The most effective manner in which you could find out your target marketplace on Snapchat would be with the useful resource of posting your Snapchat username on your one of a kind money owed on social media and inspire your intention market to characteristic you.

Include this facts on your bios on terrific social networking systems and new human beings can keep on together with you. When you submit on one in each of a kind social media bills for pronouncing your presence on Snapchat, your outreach will maintain on growing.

It isn't pretty a whole lot posting statistics approximately your Snapchat account; you ought to moreover encourage human beings to feature you. You will need to have interaction your goal marketplace. Keep posting interesting matters and provide you with new strategies to make your target audience feel concerned in what you are doing.

There are unique strategies in which you may have interaction your target market on Snapchat and you've got observed out those strategies within the preceding chapters.

Chapter 13: Snapchat Lenses, Filters and Settings

Snapchat is an app imagined to help people have amusing with their photographs and films. One of the wonderful functions of Snapchat is the lens that may be used for enhancing the wonderful of a photograph. Let us check this selection in element

Snapchat lenses are quite easy to function to images, all you need to do is press and maintain the photo and the app will automatically decide in which to area the filter. This makes your interest simpler as you do now not ought to region the filters manually. Remember that the ones filters can be located on each snaps and motion images. Some not unusual lenses used are a butterfly crown, floral wreath, face transfer, dog-ears and the rainbow one.

Filters help you write on pinnacle of a photograph or video. It moreover affords an area to function a caption or tagline. This is useful, as it will tell the opposite individual what you are trying to do in the image. Just like with a lens you can swipe proper or left to locate the clean out of choice and place it on pinnacle of the image or video. Once there, fill in some aspect you need to feature because the caption.

Check filters

It can occasionally get difficult if you have to pick among outstanding filters. For this, check every and settle for the one you determined fits the picture first rate. For example, press the show and use to vicinity filters earlier than deciding on the handiest that remains. This is high-quality for all those who can't pick amongst or more filters. You also can vicinity stickers for your images. Just click on on the emoji possibility next to the T and add it to the photograph on pinnacle.

Emojis

The emojis on Snapchat are flexible and there are numerous alternatives to choose from too. Apart from together with them on your images and films, in addition they can be brought to items to your snap shots. This method that you want no longer pin the emojis to people on my own and also can pass on items which is probably there to your photo.

This makes the photos and movement pix a bit more personal and interesting for the viewers. They may be pinned anywhere you would really like them to be in the photograph or video.

Songs

Songs and song are a huge a part of Snapchat films. They decorate the first-class and revel in of the movement photos. Although Snapchat does not have an brought audio function, it's far quite easy to embody track into your motion pictures. Record the video with the tune playing in the historical beyond and Snapchat will document and add it to the heritage.

Music

It is likewise possible at the manner to turn off the song. In order to alternate it off, document the video with the sound, as in order to be an alternative. Now you could find the amount choice at the bottom unique like a loudspeaker. Press as soon as to exchange it off and an X will seem in the the front of it to indicate that the quantity has been have come to be off. The video will now not play the sound even as it's miles regarded.

Chapter 14: Snapchat Tips and Tricks

Snapchat find out

Snapchat find out is a very specific function on Snapchat designed to help you preserve tabs on magazines, net web sites and different such channels which you need to look at. Snapchat permits in presenting all the one of a type channels and apps in a single region so that you don't must down load the man or woman apps.

Right from Cosmopolitan to Buzzfeed to MTV, there is lots to pick out out out from and clicking on them will come up with all the modern statistics and gossip. You also may be able to get proper of entry to live memories and different such fun content fabric at the identical time as not having to move away the app. You don't need to usually click on on the character apps and can press it all of the manner down to enroll inside the man or woman channels. The contemporary records from the internet site online will automatically update with out you having to manually search for it.

This characteristic makes it relatively accessible for people to keep music of all of the current occasions and happenings round them. All the abilities are professionally curated to make it appearance exquisite. You will have the chance to apply it as perception and give you top notch content material cloth fabric yourself to proportion with buddies and fans.

Updating

You have the choice to manually replace Snapchat if you want. Although it generally updates mechanically, you may manually search for any updates at the play store. Click the replace button to do the needful and your Snapchat can be up to date. If you are not able to acquire this then pass in your settings and test if you have decided on to get preserve of automatic updates. If not, then allow the selection to robotically replace your Snapchat.

Secret screenshot

You can secretly screenshot human beings's photos without them understanding something approximately it. Here are the steps to follow for the equal. Start with the resource of loading the snap but don't open it. If it has automatically loaded then do not open it. Once you load the picture, go to notifications, and turn on the plane mode. Once plane mode is on faucet the Snapchat button and opens it. Screenshot the use of the usual technique.

Now exit the app and make sure it is not taking walks within the records. IOS customers can double-click on on at the house button and swipe the app to close it. Android customers can try this in the multitasking window and close to it. Now deactivate aircraft mode and near Snapchat. You can now open Snapchat and hold on as regular.

Assign numbers

It is plain that we can have some extraordinary buddies in our lists. This refers to people who we regularly message. You have the choice of converting their numbers that permits you to message them with out troubles. Snapchat mechanically assigns numbers to the ones that you message regularly.

It commonly assigns the amount 3 but this may be modified to a five or 7 relying on what you would love to assign to it. This will make it much less complex with a purpose to message the ones humans without seeking out them in your pal list.

Deleting your account

If for some purpose you do not preference to keep your account as a consequence of security motives then you definately have the choice to delete it. Log in on your account and choose out the delete possibility. This will delete your account for precise. You may be capable of create a few other account the use of a considered one of a kind username.

However, bear in mind, after you delete your account, it can not be undone, and you can not retrieve the equal. You will ought to create a modern one with a latest username.

Travel mode

You have the choice of choosing journey mode in your Snapchat account on the manner to prevent automatic download of photos and films. This is great for all the ones whose cellphone batteries will be predisposed to drain away speedy. Performing this simple trick allow you to store on battery existence and not need to fear about undesirable pics downloading on your cellphone.

Choose those you desire to down load and get saved to your cell telephone. To permit the travel mode, go to settings and then to "manipulate." There you will discover the selection of "additional offerings" in which you can find out tour mode. Click on it to allow it.

Deleting snaps

It is viable so that you can delete a unmarried snap from a tale. This is beneficial for all those who have a tendency to feature in severa snap shots after which trim it proper all of the way down to length. For this, pick out the photograph you would like to delete and swipe it upwards. The delete button will seem on top and pressing it will eliminate that unique photograph from the tale. A pop-up will ask in case you actually need to delete the photograph and deciding on delete once more will make the snap disappear.

Content from outside Snapchat

Now you can surprise in case you are handiest allowed to feature the ones snaps and films on Snapchat that have been created the usage of Snapchat device. The answer is not any, you don't want to depend on Snapchat by myself for developing your snaps and movies. It is also possible that allows you to feature content material material material that changed into created the use of outside apps.

There are many zero.33 party apps to help you create snaps and movement photos using your virtual digicam and then keep it for your virtual digital camera roll. The identical may be uploaded in your Snapchat account.

Reusing snaps

It is possible so that it will hire antique snaps and motion images and repost them with new content fabric which includes lenses and filters. This can be beneficial for individuals who need to maintain it interesting and particular however don't have the time to take new pictures. All you have to do is faucet at the download arrow as soon due to the fact the snap has been taken.

This will store the photograph for you. If you want to down load an entire tale, then head over to the dots on the right of the tale display show display and choose out the download button to download the tale. Once finished, add any filters and lens you need or adjust it in a few other manner you want in advance than importing it.

Here are a few significant suggestions on how you can make your snaps look clean and fantastic.

Camera

First and crucial, get yourself a smartphone with a excellent top notch digital digicam. It is crucial to have a the front coping with digicam, as you will be capable of see the snap being taken. Although a first-rate back digital camera with flash can also moreover artwork, you will need to take more than one snaps to select out out the fine one.

If you may be the usage of Snapchat to promote your services and products then it is going to be exceptional to carry out a little research on the brilliant cell smartphone or tablet to pick out. You additionally have the choice of using an fantastic amazing outside digital virtual digital camera to take the images and then add to your Snapchat account.

Lighting

The subsequent component to undergo in mind is the lighting fixtures. The lighting fixtures can play a huge component in making or breaking the right photograph. You need to take the photograph in a colourful spot. However, ensure it isn't too colourful, as it will create a brilliant mild on your face. Trial and errors is a need to so you can locate the right attitude and lights to your face.

Nothing beats daylight or natural mild as it gives definitely the proper quantity of brightness. If you are attempting to photo an object then area it in the perfect place in advance than taking the picture.

Editors

Make use of editors to beautify the photograph extraordinary. There are precise out of doors applications that can be made use of for reinforcing pix. However, with Snapchat, precise editors were furnished within the app itself. These will add a piece little bit of finesse for your pix.

Filters and lens

The very last step is to utilize filters and lenses. These will assist a image appearance interesting and amusing. There are awesome filters to pick out from and they may be all amusing to apply. Choose something you observed will look wonderful.

These shape the unique standards to endure in thoughts at the equal time as taking the first-class snap.

Monetize Your Snapchat Account

These above-stated suggestions are available to be had whilst you need to monetize your account. For doing this, you want to add suitable exceptional photographs which are capable of captivate the creativeness of people and capability advertisers.

Here is how you could monetize your Snapchat account.

Step 1: The first step is to create content material in order to take preserve of the viewer's interest. This can variety from attempting on makeup products to wearing clothes and add-ons to reviewing products.

Step 2: The subsequent step might be to get positioned thru organizations in order to sponsor your pics and films.

Step three: Once they technique you, take a look at the phrases and situations they have got and undergo it all in detail. Once you are glad with it, you can sign up with them.

Step four: They will offer the basis for films and snaps they assume from you. You will must adhere to their requirements and upload the equal.

Step five: You may be paid for your paintings based totally at the settlement you have got were given with them.

This is a in fact pinnacle way to monetize when you have a massive form of fans following your Snapchat account.

Chapter 15: What exactly is Snapchat?

Snapchat is a totally powerful social media platform that has grow to be very well-known as of late. Major brands are not best starting to get their presence onto Snapchat but additionally promote it on the platform thru Snapchat's discovery device. Snapchat is much like precise social media packages in that you create a profile and then have followers or fanatics which you communicate with. However, that is pretty a high-quality deal the quantity of the similarities. Snapchat is remarkably specific in the manner that clients talk with each special and in the strategies that facts is shared.

How Snapchat Works

Snapchat is a program that works with a totally specific media for speakme with distinct clients. There are multiple variations that make this application precise and one of the most thrilling social media structures in use in recent times just like the utilization of photographs and films to talk with other people. While Twitter, Facebook and most social media structures mainly communicate with text, the handiest textual content that you may find out right here is the captions on pix and motion photographs. Another difference became Snapchat is that when you submit your pix and movies they will best very last from 1 to 10 seconds with just a unmarried exception, which we'll get into later.

It is probably tough to apprehend how this works in case you've in no manner used the utility. Just trust that someone you're following on social media posts some thing and also you get an alert. You visit their feed and test what they've posted and it's far both a photo with a caption or a quick video, or if you didn't get there speedy sufficient, you overlooked out. That's basically how Snapchat works and you've got lovers and friends at the platform just like you do with exceptional social media net sites.

What's the Point of Snapchat?

Snapchat is fundamental the manner into the future of social media. This platform goes to be one of the big ones as a way to serve the following era of consumers. The app is already being utilized by most young adults or maybe Facebook has visible the fee of Snapchat and provided $three billion for the corporation. However, the creators of Snapchat believed in their organization sufficient that they refused Facebook's offer. Facebook has those who examine a high-quality deal of facts an excellent way to assume destiny tendencies and in the event that they assume Snapchat is precious then producers need to be leaping on as fast as they're able to.

So, what's the point of Snapchat? To socialize. To assemble a following. To communicate with different individuals who percent pastimes with you or have an emotional investment in what you're posting. On one hand, Snapchat is simplest a social media platform however however it could be the utility which leads the fee into the destiny wherein social media posts may be an lousy lot less textual content and further photographs and video. Brands like Mashable, National Geographic and Comedy Central similarly to numerous dozen others see sufficient rate in Snapchat to market it with the software as a part of the discovery characteristic and masses of others have joined the platform as well. If you have got a brand – it need to be on Snapchat.

Chapter 16: Getting Your Brand on Snapchat

The first detail which you're going to need to do if you need to gain the benefits of the Snapchat utility is get your logo onto the platform. This financial disaster will deliver an reason for precisely what you need to do to create your Snapchat account and a way to fill out your profile facts effectively just so your Snapchat is ready to apply and you could begin getting lovers and advertising and marketing your brand in new and interesting strategies.

Signing up

Obviously, the number one aspect that you're going to want to do is down load the Snapchat application. You can upload this app to every your Android or your iOS device. There is not any help for Windows operating structures as of however or any of the lesser-recognized ones. Once you have got Snapchat downloaded in your phone or mobile device, launch it and also you'll be taken to a show wherein it's going to ask you to either check in or join up. You are going to sign on with the subsequent facts:

Email Address

You want to use an e mail deal with that you clearly take a look at. In reality, this may be a notable time to use your primary e mail cope with – or the most effective on your employer. Whatever you do, don't just make one up because you may must verify your account.

Password and Date of Birth

The next element that you'll input is your password and your date of shipping. There aren't many regulations along with your password and you should have no trouble coming into one. Your date of beginning is likewise smooth, the use of the date tool that consists of maximum mobile gadgets.

Your Phone Number

The very last element which you'll input is your smartphone huge variety. You want to go into your valid cellular sizable range due to the reality they will be going to ship you a verification code that you'll must enter into the app to use it truely.

Verification Code

They're going to deliver you the verification code but you can not be capable of input it into the app with out some assist navigating to the proper location. Since we are going to get into navigation in a later financial disaster, and offer an reason for in which the entirety is, for now clearly recognize that the region you input your verification code is beneath the equipment icon that opens the settings menu.

Your Profile and Logo

Snapchat doesn't have a place in an effort to fill out your profile like Twitter and Facebook and other social media systems do. In reality, you may't even add your brand from the app.

The most effective issue that you can do in case you want to customise your profile picture from the app is take a picture of either your face or a picture of your emblem and customize it that way. The trouble with this approach is that it doesn't look professional and feel Snapchat takes a series of five photos, speedy in a row to make an energetic GIF, it's far now not possible to keep your hand everyday sufficient to get a exquisite image, even when you have a high wonderful digital digital camera.

For manufacturers, that is just unacceptable. However, there may be a way to get your profile photograph to be your brand and to insert it digitally, just so it's miles as excellent as possible. We gets into that in Chapter Four.

Chapter 17: Using Snapchat the Basics

Now that you've signed up for a Snapchat and your emblem is at the app, you will want to apprehend the manner to use the software application. In this financial smash, we're high-quality going to transport over the basics – the stuff you want to apprehend to get around and check out the some of the buttons and knobs. In subsequent chapters, we are able to cover more superior capabilities and some subjects in similarly detail, along with a number of the capabilities the groups are going to be the usage of the maximum.

Navigation

The first detail which you want to recognize is a way to navigate Snapchat correctly. So go to your app and open it and examine along as we speak how you navigate through the Snapchat interface. When you enter the software, the primary thing you'll see is your virtual virtual digital camera, either going via you are going thru a protracted manner from you, relying on what you've set it at. It may be very smooth to alternate the virtual camera view. If you desired to take a selfie as an opportunity a image of what is in the the front of you, all you do is touch the little smiley face surrounded with the useful resource of arrows in the top proper of your digital digital camera show display. Is very smooth to hit this with the aid of twist of fate, it definitely is why you can see your digital digicam going through the the the front are dealing with you even as you login.

Navigating is done with swipes. If you swipe right you will see your contacts list, which might be truly group Snapchat right now. You can tap on the little speech bubble at the pinnacle right corner of the display to talk along with your contacts and you can seek them thru touching the magnifying glass. This is mainly beneficial if you have hundreds and masses of people in your touch list and also you want to discover a specific individual.

If you swipe left you could see the testimonies which have been posted. The main manufacturers – or people who have grow to be a Snapchat associate on the top row while the other recollections are from live activities beneath the phrase 'live.'

If you swipe down from your own home show show display you may see your Snapchat QR code this is the yellow icon with the ghost inside the middle. Those dots which you see there ship a message to cell devices of clients that want to look at you and make it very easy to examine a person. This is one of the contemporary new techniques of which incorporates followers the Snapchat is provide you with. As you can see there are various functions on right here. You see your trophies as an example, see who introduced you and add exclusive people and then get a listing of your buddies.

You moreover be conscious that there may be a tools icon in the top proper nook. Tapping this may will will let you view your private information and if you scroll down you'll see the login verification placing. This is wherein you will input the code that they sent you through your mobile device. If you selected no longer to add a cellphone quantity they have you ever ever treatment a puzzle rather to expose which you're individual.

That is all are going to cover for now. We gets into the extra advanced features in the subsequent couple chapters. If you are a brand and you want a quick start assist manual to get you on Snapchat as fast as viable, the following financial disaster covers the skills that organizations want to apprehend.

Chapter 18: Using Snapchat Features Businesses Use the Most

As cited inside the final financial ruin, we are now going to head over a couple of the features that agencies use the most, mainly the emblem and QR code. This is meant as type of a brief begin process. The basics in the very last chapter had been speculated to get you navigating throughout the software software successfully and this financial catastrophe will show a way to apply your QR code and a workaround for the dearth of functionality to function your logo's emblem to your profile immediately.

Your Logo and QR Code

Adding your logo in your Snapchat is going to take some creativity. That's due to the fact Snapchat doesn't assist you to add a brand. What it does allow you to do is take in photo – that is truly a series of five snap shots taken one proper after the opportunity – of your face or something you need. So, you could take a photo of your logo and it's going to probably be on your Snapchat profile and QR code. You want to both find out a way to take a image with the digital digital digital camera this is flawlessly even though – and in reality high first-rate – or give you a few modern way to take a picture of your logo with the 5 snapshots in case you want to be strung together to make a short GIF.

As for your QR code, it is intended to be a few detail which you percent in the actual international and allow humans to take snap shots of to feature you on Snapchat. You can add your emblem to your QR code image that you need to be cautious doing it so that you don't mess up the code embedded within the dots that lets in Snapchat to recognize your emblem from that QR code.

The first detail which you're going to do is download your QR code, which calls if you need to visit that hyperlink (this is the Snapchat internet web site), login in your Snapchat account after which down load your QR code. Then, you could both take it into

Photoshop your self (and Photoshop is normally recommended for this particular venture due to the layers characteristic) and magically erase the white ghost after which placed your brand on the layer underneath it honestly so it is able to be seen through the transparency of the ghost. You can also discover a person on Fiverr to do it for you if you don't have Photoshop or don't want to use it. There are a few pretty specific pointers which you want to take a look at but, and if you're outsourcing this assignment, make certain which you percentage those with the person.

Do no longer modify the shape of the ghost and do now not harm the black border. (Or do away with it) all through the ghost. This will cause your QR code to fail and people will now not be capable of use it to observe you on Snapchat.

Don't stretch the field and except for trade the shape of it.

Don't invert the colours to try to be amazing.

Do no longer print on glossy paper or cardstock because of the reality the shine also can save you people from the ones days, scanning your code.

Then, you simply positioned up the QR code anywhere you want – your internet internet site on line, social media systems and anywhere on line, however additionally in the real global. You can also need to have the QR code blown up and published on the wall at your brick-and-mortar keep(s), you could even located it in your commercial business enterprise gambling playing cards. You would in all likelihood additionally be able to located it on a billboard or at the problem of agency automobiles, however you ought to check that very well in advance than spending any big amount of money on it.

There are other functions that groups use, which encompass the story characteristic, but we're going to get into that assignment in Chapters Six and Eight.

Chapter 19: Using Snapchat Advanced Features

In this financial spoil, we're going to head over a number of the extra advanced skills of Snapchat. We're going to skip topics to be able to be included in later chapters like testimonies however this financial disaster will can help you use the number one features of Snapchat much like the movies and pics to get you began in the platform's international.

Using Zoom in Your Videos

You don't ought to take a wellknown picture or video with Snapchat. By default, the movies is zoomed all the manner out however all you need to do to zoom in is find arms and pull them aside similar to in case you are zooming in on an internet internet website on your phone. Zooming out is the alternative; carry your palms together. One unique small factor observe: if you haven't observed it however, the manage to flip your digicam from the front-going through to rear-going through is at the pinnacle proper of your video display.

Using Your Own Photos

In case you didn't understand, you could use the photos which might be on your cellphone's library to apply in a single-to-one verbal exchange in a right away message. All you do is swipe proper on any friend which you need to ship a picture to and tap on the blue bubble at the left facet of the display screen at the same time as it comes in the frame. Your private chat will open with them and you may tap at the yellow circle including you're getting ready to take a picture, and whilst your camera comes up, have a look at the lowest right wherein you will see the closing photograph which you took and you can faucet on it and open your library. Then insert a few component picture from your library you need and percentage it as a snap.

Improving Your Snaps and Videos

You probably already understand that you may add a caption in your photo video. After all, the app from time to time asks you in case you want to move away a caption on the identical time as you click on on the shutter button; (if it doesn't, you can click on at the 'T' at the top). But did there are in truth strategies that you can decorate your caption? Here are the processes that you may make your snaps and movies look notable.

You can change the scale of your caption text further to the placement. All you need to do is after you type your caption, kind the 'T' a 2nd time and it will make your text a bargain larger and thicker. If you tap it once more, it's going to middle your textual content. If you need to make your text even huge then use the identical spreading your palms movement which you used to zoom and make it as big as you need. Make nice that you positioned each finger at the end of the text; it can take some practice attempts. You can then take a look at with shifting the textual content round and resizing it to create a few thing you want.

You probably saw the icon that looks like a chunk of paper to the left of the textual content icon, and the only on the right that seems like a pencil or pen. The one on the left is the entire listing of emojis that Snapchat has to provide. You can select an emoji, and then resize it similar to you in all likelihood did with the textual content further to pass it round, rotate it or something you want. If you tap on the pencil icon at permits you to choose a colour after which write collectively with your finger (or a stylus if you have one) for your snap. You can discover a listing of the emojis and what they imply on-line.

Another factor that you could do is go to your settings menu and switch on geofilters. All you do is move all the manner all the way down to extra offerings and faucet manage and it'll can help you permit filters. Once you have got finished this you may move once more for your photo and it will ask you – or as an opportunity assist you to apprehend – that you can swipe right for filters. Filters variety with each geographical sector it is why

Snapchat asked on your ZIP Code whilst you allow them. Go through the filters which might be to be had and word if there any you need.

There are more than one neat topics that you can try this we're able to give up the chapter with. First, if you faucet at the phrases on your caption you may be conscious that tapping on one phrase will underline it then you could tap the word and maintain and it will spotlight it. Then you could alternate the colour of that character phrase to anything you need. This is specially useful if you want to apply letters as frames. You can play with this and discover what works exceptional for you but an instance is making the 'O' massive sufficient to in which maximum of it's far out of body and the detail that is left frames your photo in an oval. Finally, any other advanced function which you ought to recognize approximately is that when steady with day you can replay someone's snap. However, it wishes to be the very last snap that you seemed. You will see the selection to replay on your display after the snap expires.

Chapter 20: Marketing on Snapchat

Marketing on Snapchat is a hint uncommon and it's far centered around the tale function. We receives into the actual manufacturing of stories in Chapter 8; the motive of this bankruptcy is to reveal you how you market with tales.

The first component you ought to realise is what a tale absolutely is. That calls for expertise a touch bit of Snapchat terminology in case you haven't already determined out it. A snap is a video or photograph that you supply a specific character. Although you in reality can put it on the market with snaps, they'll be only going to as a minimum one person at a time and they disappear in no greater than 10 seconds. This makes it an nearly unusable advertising device – however the fact that it had been worthwhile to deliver snaps for your gift friends list. Of course, it's no longer profitable and that's the point. So, we received't fear approximately snaps in this financial disaster.

However, we're going to talk approximately reminiscences. The distinction between a story and a snap is that memories include more than one snap shots and video and live available for viewing for twenty-four hours. The unique distinction is that at the same time as you can send snaps to genuinely humans on your pals listing (or the unusual person this is enabled honestly every body to deliver them snaps) you stories may be considered with the resource of absolutely everyone you choose. You can set your account to permit all people to view your memories. Since reminiscences can be shared, they may be a tremendous advertising and marketing and marketing and advertising and marketing approach.

Setting Your Account so Everyone Can View Your Stories

This is a few issue, as you can have guessed, that may be completed for your settings menu. So swipe down and on the identical time as you get to the internet web page

114

wherein it lets in you to see who has delivered you, click on at the settings equipment at the top right. Then flow all the way down to in which you can change every who can ship you snaps and who can view your tales.

So now you're organized to start sharing stories on Snapchat. You may not realise the way to construct a tale however, but that's adequate due to the reality are going to cover that during Chapter 8. Make high quality that you allow special social media networks apprehend while you located up a tale due to the truth you can have Snapchat customers on the ones networks and they will log in and test out your tale. If your story is geared closer to three sort of products or services you genuinely need as many human beings viewing it as feasible, so don't depend upon definitely Snapchat to get views. However, maintain in mind to constantly be specific in order that customers will want to share your tale with others, and could come lower back for the subsequent one.

Chapter 21: Getting Your Initial Following

If you need to achieve fulfillment in advertising on Snapchat then you truely're going to want to get a following. Just like together with your Twitter and Facebook lovers, the more humans that you have following you, the better the chances that unique human beings will comply with you. This bankruptcy will give you some hints on getting your first lovers on Snapchat further to three subjects not to do to get fans.

Let Your Creativity Free

The first aspect that you want to do is make sure that a few thing which you're posting is modern and a laugh and indicates off your innovative expressions. Posting stupid content fabric with textual content that is constantly the identical in no way modifications, over the identical stupid movies of merchandise are going to get exactly nowhere with Snapchat. But pictures of people the usage of your product in unconventional strategies, with your caption and emojis, goes to get humans's interest and cause them to want to share your content material fabric.

Use Your Other Social Networks

We referred to this a piece bit inside the final monetary disaster however it might be beneficial to recognize precisely the manner you need to use your social networks to get Snapchat fans. The super manner to do it is to offer you compelling matters to post to your Twitter, Facebook, Instagram or something social community you're using. These are teaser devices which incorporates a promo code within the tale that you may first-rate get in case you go to Snapchat.

Put Your Snapcode Everywhere

Place your snapcode or Snapchat data anywhere that you may. Post it in your website, round your keep when you have one and everywhere else that you may consider wherein human beings which you need to persuade might be inclined to join Snapchat or are already using it. You furthermore positioned it for your commercial enterprise playing cards, put a link to it on your electronic mail or maybe market it on boards which might be for your enterprise.

Use Social Media Influencers

Do a YouTuber or someone who has a massive following on line however isn't necessarily Hollywood movie star? Do you trust you studied they're a person that might be interested in your products or services? You might be capable of leverage influencers via supplying them some thing unique which they will almost constantly speak approximately in a while and you may get lovers from that.

Things Not to Do to Get Followers on Snapchat

There are a few subjects that you shouldn't do to get fans on Snapchat. One of them is to apply one of the offerings furnished on internet web web sites like Fiverr that promise to get you hundreds of fanatics. For one issue, they will be not going to shop for some component from you and might not even have real people in the again of them. Also, you can get your Snapchat account banned via using doing so subsequently in the destiny. You also should strive no longer to be stupid and make sure which you're reachable in some way because of the truth clients don't want a shadowy face within the background, they need a real live man or girls behind your enterprise that they might interact with.

Chapter 22: Building Fans via Stories

You're going to apply memories to do greater than promote it your services or products. Think of a tale like a viral video. You recognize if you make it overly promotional it's no longer going to paintings. You need a few aspect smart, something that no person has ever seen and some thing that inspires emotion in someone or ladies. This will cause them to need to percentage with their buddies and it will come up with the publicity that you're looking for. But growing actual reminiscences may additionally even make human beings need to comply with you so whenever you create a story preserve in mind which you are every searching for to get humans to conform with you and also you're in search of to get your products or services to be had.

Creating Amazing Stories

If you want to apprehend the manner to create a excellent Snapchat tale then log on and have a have a look at a number of the great ones which have ever been made. There are plenty of Snapchat reminiscences that have been featured on web web sites like Buzzfeed, Mashable or even a number of the extra traditional media out there. As you leaf through those Snapchat testimonies and chortle, attempt to remember techniques in which you can contain a comparable marketing marketing campaign to your very personal Snapchat account that might each be precise and promote your services or products a bit.

Stories cannot simplest be told in images, they also can encompass video. You can offer you with a smart idea to pair the video with the snapshots if you want. There are lots of strategies to create a brilliant story but it starts offevolved with an outstanding concept. Sit down with personnel or maybe your pals and attempt to give you a Snapchat story that might be funny. Use some thing for concept; visit Google search and type in a random word and take a look at the pics that offer you with that word. Look spherical your surroundings and see if there's whatever there that amuses you. Think about the very last issue that you discovered humorous and why you preferred it. There are lots of methods to come up with top notch thoughts for memories.

Sit down and storyboard out your story, due to this that making a decision which order your snaps and movies are going to transport in, in advance than you even take them in some instances, after which make sure that you have the right order and a compelling tale this is going to keep humans clicking the subsequent button. Remember, much like with YouTube films, you shouldn't skip over a few minutes in period. Otherwise, human beings are going to become bored. Now, you could get to work making exceptional memories on Snapchat!

Chapter 23: Discover Snapchat's Partner Program

One trouble you may be interested by knowledge about is Snapchat's associate software known as Discover. This application is quite a wonderful deal out of reap for each person who isn't a major brand because of the $750,000 (in step with day) price tag, but there are in truth other techniques to get on Discover then with the aid of being a accomplice with Snapchat.

Some of the foremost manufacturers are letting exclusive brands promote it on their Discover area for masses an lousy lot a great deal much less than they may be paying for their Discover spot. This is a manner for the manufacturers which is probably advertising and advertising on Discover to get a number of the cash over again that they may be spending and it's far a extraordinary way for every body with approximately $50,000 to spend to get a big amount of publicity.

For smaller brands, regrettably there may be not anything but that they could do to start advertising and advertising with Snapchat. There can also want to must be some type of essential overhaul to the software within the occasion that they have been going to begin allowing human beings to promote it on snaps and motion snap shots and different places throughout the internet site. Right now, there is not anything this is the equal of Facebook advertising and marketing and advertising for small companies and those with products or services to sell but that may be coming within the future. Snapchat has only currently been able to get sufficient lovers to command the shape of quotes that they'll be getting from their Discover software.

So the lowest line right right here is, if you have a notable deal of cash to spend on advertising and advertising then Snapchat can be precisely what you need – or at the least advertising and advertising and marketing on one of the manufacturers which is probably currently on or might be on Snapchat's Discover software in the near future. If you have a small commercial enterprise corporation in any other case you simply need to market it products and services, then you definitely definately definately need to use Snapchat for advertising capabilities inside the techniques that we mentioned on this e-book in region of advertising at the platform.

Chapter 24: Viewing Statistics

Another component that you're going to need to do what it involves Snapchat is find out what form of facts you could get and the way you can use them to make your emblem higher. Unfortunately Snapchat doesn't in reality offer any shape of real analytics or some issue to inform you who's journeying your story web page, but it does have some records which you would possibly find beneficial. In this newsletter were going to move over the ones in addition to inform you approximately the alternatives which is probably cropping up which can offer you with the analytics records which you want.

There are several metrics that Snapchat gives you. The first one that we're going to speak approximately here is the general precise views that a story has gotten – and memories are the only analytics that we can talk right here due to the truth that's what you will be the use of as a marketer and it also includes the handiest characteristic on the net internet web page that Snapchat gives analytics on.

126

Total precise perspectives will let you recognize how many humans opened up your tale and saw at the least the primary frame. They may not of prolonged lengthy long gone on to complete the tale and in fact might not have even if past that first frame but it tells you what number of humans opened up your tale and it is very correct. The thing approximately recollections is that you can see how many views are on each single body of the story – or on the video in case you created a video – and that's the way you get the ones commonplace precise perspectives – you go to the number one frame and look.

The 2d analytic which have been going to speak about is enormous story completions. You get your wellknown tale completions thru going to the very last frame of your story and taking a glance how many human beings finished your tale. Make positive which you're preserving music of those metrics as you see them and moreover hold in thoughts is this can be after the 24 hours that your story has been stay.

The 1/3 analytic might be the maximum important of all of those and it's the finishing touch charge which you'll parent out your self via using looking at your preferred specific views in assessment to your typical story completions. So as an example, if you had one thousand human beings start your story but fine 450 finished it you may have a 45% very last contact fee; the better that your price is, the higher your tale.

Finally, the fourth analytic that were going to speak approximately is the preventing issue. You want to test your snaps and try to determine out if there may be a style as to when they stopped searching or viewing your story. If you can discover a fashion at a sure frame then you may have positioned in which the hassle have grow to be – which means that the problem changed into someplace as an entire lot as that element not continuously the body that they stopped on.

Companies That Are Providing Analytics Information

There are a few companies available that are offering analytics statistics for Snapchat. They have handiest popped up presently, however they've got a few innovative applications and severa have notable reputations with agencies that are on the lookout for to marketplace on Snapchat. If you want to find out what is going on along with your Snapchat account and feature focused analytics so you may need to make the first-class picks feasible on what to place up and on the same time as similarly to what's working and what isn't, then you definitely clearly could in all likelihood want to analyze using this type of organizations. Just do your studies and make sure that different human beings are recommending the issuer and that the charge isn't outrageous in contrast to the going price.

Chapter 25: Using Snapchat at Live Events to get Followers

In this financial ruin, had been going to talk about multiple techniques that you can use live activities to get fans on your Snapchat account. The first issue that you have to do is open up your Snapchat app and appearance in which the Discover page is. You will see an area in which it says live after which you could discover recollections beneath that. Don't get pressured thru way of this stay occasion feature that Snapchat has.

They do a component referred to as Our Story wherein they choose a live occasion that's taking area and then take people's snaps and video from that occasion and gather a curated story that everybody can see regardless of who they're following. That isn't the kind of live event so one can be discussing in this bankruptcy. The form of live event that you want to use Snapchat for is the shape of live event in which your agency commercial enterprise business enterprise is doing some thing exciting that clients can attend. You can maintain those sports on every occasion you like, and you can use Snapchat to every deliver people in your stay event and convince humans which may be already at your live event to join up and observe you on Snapchat.

The manner which you get people out of your Snapchat for your stay event in all fairness sincere. Just assemble a story the usage of snaps in that occasion and invite humans out. Just don't forget, recollections final for twenty-four hours so the exceptional way with the intention to do a live event with Snapchat testimonies is have the story begin before the live event begins – 24 hours earlier than the begin of your occasion. Then you can begin a brand-new tale while the event starts offevolved offevolved offevolved and people can be in a position to test out stay photographs and video from the occasion.

Obviously, that may be a brilliant way to get human beings on your event due to the truth you not nice get humans that must prepare for the event and are inclined to go back 24 hours after being attentive to about it, however you furthermore mght get folks that are more of proper-proper right right here-right-now, fly thru the seat of your pants humans. In particular phrases, individuals who will come in your stay event on very brief observe.

It is well properly well worth noting that this may fine art work if you have fans in the identical town that you are doing the event in and in case you are a huge brand and you are in a huge city that is usually now not a trouble. For small businesses, lots of their enthusiasts ought to have followed them by way of manner of getting into their brick-and-mortar store and so they may no longer have a trouble both.

Chapter 26: Using Snapchat to Deliver Personal Content

This financial disaster is designed to offer you some thoughts on how you can supply personal content cloth to the the ones who have a have a look at you on Snapchat, which incorporates what shape of content material material cloth you may supply and some thoughts for a few first rate private deliveries, in addition to tips at the way you want to supply them.

This is something that you may do in my opinion together with your enthusiasts and is designed to paintings with a merchandising which you have going on. For example, anticipate that you posted in your internet internet web page that sooner or later within the next few days you'll provide away a fantastic amount of free gadgets or gift certificate however that the individuals who must get maintain of them will be fanatics on Snapchat whom you despatched a private snap to.

What you have to do next, is choose out a specific day throughout that week or even choose the hours that you may be doing it amongst. Then you could ramp up your advertising efforts a hint at some stage in that length because of the truth that the human beings which may be following you on Snapchat are paying hobby because they need to get a unfastened object and they'll look at your stories more often. This is honestly one manner that handing over non-public content material cloth can help your employer.

Another manner that you could use private touch to make bigger your industrial enterprise is with the resource of thanking customers when they purchase some thing from your internet site through sending them a snap and then create a story with the ones snaps. This is a superb method because all it calls for is which you asked humans in your order form to install their Snapchat ID.

There are many unique strategies available of the use of private conversation to develop your enterprise. You can try to get referrals from the those who are currently following you with the aid of making a tale that tells them that they will get something at a huge cut price or freed from charge if they could get a certain wide kind of human beings to have a look at you on Snapchat. You might also moreover need to have them submit on a few different social media community – Twitter is the great opportunity – due to the truth you can now not see it on Snapchat within the event that they snap and ship you the decision of someone that discovered you based mostly on their advice. You can ask them to submit the person's Snapchat ID on Twitter with a particular hashtag and then you can check your Snapchat lovers to find out if that person has joined that day after which you may then deliver them credit score rating for the take a look at.

Chapter 27: Give Followers an Inside Look

Another exceptional way that you could use Snapchat is to provide your lovers with a few at the back of-the-scenes data or an indoors have a take a look at some thing which you're doing. This has a number of blessings, first and essential being that the folks who comply with you on Snapchat pays closer interest for your snaps and tales and will hold your commercial enterprise in thoughts in the event that they need your services or products due to the fact you're already of their thoughts. But every other advantage is that during case you're behind the scenes data is exciting, and something you're building or doing is compelling, human beings are going to need to percent it.

There are loads of methods that you may use this. First of all, make sure that each one of the alternative social media you operate knows that you're posting one-of-a-kind scenes data on Snapchat. That manner that if the fans from your one-of-a-kind social media structures want to see the in the returned of-the-scenes facts, they'll be going to become fans on Snapchat as nicely, which offers you extra fans. You can use this numerous approaches to get fans every time you have something that you may display behind the scenes facts of.

You might also even strain website online site visitors on your private net website online the use of Snapchat. If you snap and assemble testimonies you may place a way for buying in your net internet site online inside the tale further to a purpose for them to move there – a call to motion this is going to offer them a few shape of benefit. You usually want to ensure that you have a few type of benefit to offer them. One wonderful manner to use Snapchat to get some lengthy-time period effects is to direct them for your internet site and feature them join up on your mailing listing. That technique that you could now deliver emails and people will have a have a have a look at an e-mail a whole lot longer than they may a tweet or a snap story most of the time.

The most critical detail right proper right here is that you simply make sure which you are typically interacting on the aspect of your target market. If you've got got some thing that you suppose that might be superb on Snapchat, make certain you positioned it on there. Make positive which you take each opportunity which you need to deliver humans that observe you on social media a few sort of indoors records approximately your organization or a few issue that they didn't have earlier than. If you want them to do a little element and observe a call to movement, then make certain that you are supplying some kind of benefit to accomplish that as well.

Chapter 28: Running Contests & Promotions on Snapchat

Snapchat is a exquisite location to run contests and promotions. Many of the alternative agencies which can be on Snapchat use this approach to each say thanks – normally with discounts – and to get greater lovers with the resource of stirring up a few pleasure. So, how do you run a competition or merchandising at the way to do nicely on Snapchat? In this financial ruin, we'll discover a number of the strategies that you can use this shape of advertising on Snapchat and some of the blessings that you could get from it.

Designing Your Promotion

The first trouble you're going to want to do is layout your promoting. You want to determine out what type of things are going to require from the customers or fans and how you may set it up logistically. For example, they will upload you as a friend on Snapchat after which you could request them to create a video or take a picture and supply it to you.

Promoting Your Promotion

Now you're going to promote your contest. You can sell it to your brick-and-mortar maintain, to your very personal internet site and on the alternative social media systems that you use. There are all kinds of approaches that you may promote your contest but you do need to keep in thoughts that you have to permit your fanatics recognize in a completely clear style if you make a decision to apply their movies in a while in a future marketing.

Checking Your Contest Entries

The next step in the approach is checking your contest entries. For example, in case you had your clients deliver you movies one of the matters that you could do to make sure which you see all of the entries is to apply a third-birthday celebration software to view the films and store them for your cellphone. You are probably conscious via manner of now that in case you use Snapchat and a person sends you a video or a snap, it's miles going to self-destruct in no more than 10 seconds till they assemble a tale with it wherein case it is going to be lengthy beyond in 24 hours.

From there's only a rely of identifying who the winner is for your promotion or but you designed it – with multiple winners or with absolutely everyone receiving some shape of promotional code – but you pick out to create a fun and exciting advertising and marketing that your fans will like. If you may do this, you may discover that the fans which you have can be an lousy lot extra apt to check out your snaps and movies as well as testimonies on the identical time as you located up them.

Chapter 29: Aligning Yourself with Niche Influencers on Snapchat

One of the methods that you could now not have taken into consideration advertising and advertising and advertising your business enterprise organisation with Snapchat is to use location of hobby influencers. This is truely a tried-and-proper approach of advertising and advertising and it's miles some component that huge agencies do pretty regularly. Some corporations have partnered with YouTube stars in the beyond who art work inside the same place of interest as them — such is splendor groups pairing up with noticeably well-known make-up academic YouTubers — and so it is a brilliant way to marketplace your business enterprise.

What are Niche Influencers?

So, what are area of interest influencers? They are people who have loads of have an impact on over a large amount of ability clients inner your very personal area of interest. Niche influencers often have large followings that exit and buy their advocated products and agree with them implicitly. When it entails anything that they use in my opinion, fans will exit and purchase that precise product in droves, this is why producers ship famous YouTubers unfastened samples in their products all the time.

Benefits of Using Niche Influencers

There are a number of advantages to using area of hobby influencers. For one factor, you will have a chance to lure their goal marketplace to head back over on your specific company when they want a products or services that you provide. For any other, the name of your organisation might be going spherical inner circles that make up your company.

How to Use Niche Influencers

So, how need to use place of hobby influencers? There are many progressive strategies that you may do this. Some human beings deliver them free samples of some element products or services that they're promoting – as long as that precise influencer is for your agency that is perfectly proper – and others do things like permitting a famous individual to take over a social media account. In fact this is a few factor this is been pretty a style in recent times.

How to Find Niche Influencers

Finding niche influencers inner your specific enterprise isn't all that difficult. You can use internet web sites like Klout, Peer Index and Cred or any of the opportunity barometers of affect which are available. You can also test social media and find out who has a massive following inner your particular business enterprise. There are diverse strategies to head approximately this counting on what social media systems that you use but you actually ought to check Twitter, Insta Graham, Pinterest and Facebook. Of course, you may be capable of find out who the area of hobby influencers are internal your business enterprise which might be additionally on Snapchat.

Chapter 30: Measuring Your Success with Snapchat

So how do you diploma your success with Snapchat? Knowing whether or not or not or now not a advertising marketing campaign became a achievement, will rely upon growing with modern methods that you may determine out whether or not or now not some thing labored. For instance, if you did a Snapchat advertising marketing marketing marketing campaign and also you requested the clients on that platform to perform a little element on a one-of-a-type platform, then it might be very easy to degree your success – or at least the numbers. However, there may be greater to achievement than the numbers and we'll get into that right here.

First, Let's talk approximately the Numbers

Obviously, the numbers are vital. But there's a terrific deal extra to be aware of. Before you could get into any of that but, you want to recognize the numbers and so you are going to have to offer you with some technique of identifying how many humans you reached on Snapchat and the manner lots of them took your name to movement and actually take a look at through with signing up for an electronic mail listing, posting a tweet with a positive hashtag or something precise method that you are using. You can appoint the Snapchat device that have been mentioned inside the bankruptcy on analytics further for your very very own strategies of counting humans that have spoke back.

Now, Let's Talk about the Demographics

So, you may need to decide out a few way that you may get demographic statistics from the humans which might be responding in your advertising campaigns. Demographics are tremendous critical when it comes to campaigns because in case you understand what shape of humans have spoke back to a particular service or product, or advertising and marketing advertising and marketing campaign, then you sincerely recognize the manner to beautify it next time.

Demographics may be tough to get within the extraordinary way might be to go with one of the organizations which have been stated inside the bankruptcy on analytics due to the fact there can be without a doubt no manner to get that statistics along facet your non-public efforts.

Now, Let's Talk approximately User Response

The closing problem which you want to degree is how the users felt about the specific advertising and advertising and marketing advertising and marketing campaign which you did. You need to recognise what they concept of the advertising and marketing and advertising campaign itself and additionally, you need to try and discover whether or not they had been happy to enroll in your mailing listing because of the truth the provide emerge as wonderful or whether or not they were at the fence about it. Finding out how clients responded to a particular advertising and marketing and marketing marketing advertising campaign can bypass an prolonged way in helping you enhance destiny advertising and marketing and advertising and marketing and advertising campaigns and get better responses.

Chapter 31: Learning From Other Brands on Snapchat

You want to in reality studies from one-of-a-type brands on Snapchat. There are severa tactics to do this however with the platform constantly evolving and with new advertising and marketing ideas coming all the time it is able to be a bit time-ingesting to preserve up with the whole thing. However you do need to take some time to try to figure out what exclusive companies are doing – particularly the biggest businesses because of the reality those are going to be the right ones to discover and could save you a piece time. Figure out what different brands did after which provide you with strategies that paintings just as nicely. In this bankruptcy, were going to offer you a few methods that you may find out what amazing manufacturers are up to and research from them.

News Articles

If you comply with advertising information, you are genuinely going to discover humans speakme about Snapchat. With 2 million energetic customers in keeping with month there are a whole lot of people with their eye on this precise software who want to look in which it is going – in particular due to the truth the corporation refused Facebook's provide. So if you study the advertising statistics internet sites wherein you installation your new look for Snapchat you need to assemble a find out some fantastic statistics on what some of the important manufacturers are as a good deal as almost about Snapchat.

Ask Other People within the Industry

Another detail that you can do is ask distinct humans which you understand are within the corporation. Regular communique with specialists like your self which might be inside the equal corporation which you are in will permit you to percentage a super deal of facts with every other that you could not have had to your private. People which might be inner your private enterprise are clean to discover and except they may be direct competitor there probable going to be very happy to talk approximately their techniques.

Follow Marketing Blogs That Are All about the Trends

Find some notable marketing blogs which have suited facts and then be a part of as much as get normal updates or an RSS feed from them. Bloggers will do quite a piece of studies frequently and so they will be capable of get information earlier than you could on a number of the dispositions which is probably taking vicinity in Snapchat. You can use Google looking for to discover bloggers who pay interest especially on Snapchat and at the advertising and advertising that is going with it.

Chapter 32: Integrating with Your Site & Social Media

Depending upon what form of internet web site on line you have were given, inclusive of Snapchat to it may be very easy or can be quite tough. There are such pretty a few systems to be had now for growing a net internet site online and content material cloth manage systems like WordPress aren't the simplest game enthusiasts within the DIY worldwide of internet web page introduction. In this financial disaster, had been going to speak about how you may combine Snapchat together with your internet net web page and collectively in conjunction with your social media.

If you have got got got a WordPress internet web web page being capable of integrate Snapchat will depend on the issue rely which you have. While all of the cutting-edge topics genuinely have locations for Facebook, Twitter, Pinterest and others which can be more well-known, not very among the challenge matters to be had have automated places in which you may positioned your Snapchat facts. However, you may placed your Snapchat ID or even your QR code at the sidebar of your WordPress web web page via using a text widget.

If your website is constituted of scratch with HTML then you can ought to get your web style clothier to create an area to your Snapchat QR code and for the man or woman facts that you need to put up for your net website. You have to simply located the QR code inside the header of your homepage in order that human beings can without troubles take a photograph of it and try and observe you on Snapchat on every occasion they visit your internet site.

Integrating your Snapchat into your social media is going to take some creativity to your element. There actually isn't any place that you could submit your QR code and Snapchat facts on Twitter. The handiest thing that you can do is replace your profile photo along with your QR code however this is probably a horrible idea for numerous motives – one Twitter might not be satisfied which you're the usage of a competing social media internet site's QR code on their web website on line and Snapchat might not be glad about it each.

There is also the fact that you need to have a outstanding profile picture for your Twitter account. One idea that may work on each Twitter and Facebook is setting your QR code inside the historic beyond – in twitter which means that the ancient past that your tweets are sitting on and on Facebook you would need to positioned it inside the large header profile.

Chapter 33: Why You Need to Sit Up and Take Notice of Snapchat

Snapchat is the big social community that too regularly receives not noted. Bloggers and organizations now recognise the importance of social media advertising and marketing and advertising and marketing but their mistake is in questioning that this constantly way Facebook and Twitter.

In reality despite the fact that, the important difficulty to a superb social media advertising marketing campaign is to be everyin which. And more important although, it is to be in the proper region for your particular emblem and your precise plans. If you may match the proper message with the right channel, then you may in truth assure your fulfillment and notice your logo in reality take off and take flight.

And Snapchat certainly deserves its place on your plans – specially in case you are growing a 'non-public logo' otherwise you in any other case want a terrific way to have interaction collectively together with your fanatics in a very direct and certainly non-public manner.

Because virtually, Snapchat just happens to be one of the most direct styles of marketing and one of the most private procedures to speak with an target marketplace. It has its limitations, certain, however for the right business it can be an sincerely treasured tool that converts pretty not like some different channel in

the area...

The Objections

So sincerely why is it that such pretty some people overlook the importance of Snapchat? Why is it that the social network in no manner pretty gets the identical quantity of love and attention as something like Facebook?

five

It comes proper all the way down to the way that Snapchat works, which prevents it from being an proper away apparent preference in terms of accomplishing and communicating along side your purpose marketplace. That's due to the truth Snapchat is largely 'one to at least one'. That is to say, that it allows you to message a person with a picture proper away however that picture received't be seen on any shape of feed or wall. This makes it greater comparable to non-public messaging (ala Whatsapp) rather than social advertising and marketing and advertising and marketing (ala Facebook).

The query this is on all and sundry's lips is: how do you pass approximately building an target market? How do you market to folks that aren't already following you?

This is why they could't see the rate in Snapchat and it's why it so frequently receives omitted for distinct methods.

But now reconsider that objection for a 2nd. Because sincerely, you may make the correct same argument inside the path of e-mail advertising and marketing! And as we apprehend, email advertising and marketing

158

and marketing and advertising and advertising and marketing is sincerely one of the unmarried maximum vital gadget that any marketer has at their disposal.

You could also make this argument in the direction of telemarketing – a way that efficaciously each business organization makes use of to a point or extraordinary.

And then there's the compelling stats…

The Power of Snapchat

So Snapchat works surely the equal way that electronic mail works – you construct your audience and then you definately surely use Snapchat to engage with them and to put together them in your income.

But why select out Snapchat over exclusive techniques? Or in addition to them for that count number variety?

1 It's non-public

Well for starters, Snapchat is pretty private. Snapchat works very similarly to stay streaming in this enjoy because it lets in humans to get insight into what you're doing at any given 2d. When you ship a snap, it's miles going to be received right away and maximum human beings will open it then and there. This technique that they'll see what you're presently doing and they'll realise that you definitely sent that correspondence. In this revel in, it's very similar to getting a text or a non-public message. And while that message is coming from a emblem that you virtually love, that's pretty thrilling!

2 The engagement is notable

What's greater, is that a Snapchat has fantastic engagement. And there are lots of first-rate reasons for this. For one, human beings selected to conform with you on Snapchat because of this they've given you permission to the touch them – a totally vital idea.

At the identical time, your message will show on their cellular device as a notification and they'll be capable of acquire it everywhere they are. This is partly

right of an electronic mail but best in element due to the fact often e-mail notifications sincerely say some issue like '3 New Emails' which occasionally compels us to open the app. If you're some aspect like me, it might as an alternative say '3898789 New Emails'...

Finally, Snapchat manner sending a video or an image. This is a enormously consumable format and the duration is restrained with the aid of way of nature. This manner that people who wouldn't be to sit down down and examine thru an e mail can be in a feature to test your Snapchat video and recognize it's first-class going to last more than one seconds. Or they might check the photograph.

In quick, all of this has mixed to a platform with some of the incredible engagement of any platform to be had. According to an editorial on the Huffington Post, Snapchat messages have an open price of 90% or more. So if you have 1,000 fans, you could anticipate

900 of them to open your Snapchat message! This is in evaluation to email open fees which can be as little as 25%

at their very best.

This is also an lousy lot better than Facebook or Twitter. And specially now that best 10% of your Facebook fans can see your posts on their homefeed until you pay for extra publicity!

three It's persuasive

Lots of human beings open Snapchat messages but what's extra is that they'll possibly pay attention to them. That's due to the fact they may regularly be pictures and every now and then be movies, each of that permits you to have the energy to be very in keeping withsuasive and to potentially pressure earnings.

This is a few issue that you could do plenty better in a video than you can do in writing. In a video, humans can see your body language, they might concentrate your ardour and you could use tune and one-of-a-kind pointers to in reality hammer home a element. As they may be saying: an image tells a thousand terms. And a video tells even extra!

4 Its exciting

Snapchat messages are frequently funny. Sometimes they're very insightful. And there's constantly the exhilaration of having a message with the intention to 'self-destruct' much like the start of Mission Impossible. So on the equal time as an e-mail may appear silly, a Snapchat is something you'll regularly want to check out.

And now with the filters (which with the aid of the way are specially viral in their very nature) and numerous extremely good new gear, it's becoming an increasing number of thrilling.

Facebook glaringly knew this too, seeing as it become to begin with interested in looking for the social community for a whopping

$three billion. That's extra than it paid for Oculus!

And while Mark Zuckerberg thinks an app is nicely sincerely really worth looking... it's properly properly worth searching!

Chapter 34: How to do Snapchat Marketing The Basics

So with all that during mind, how do you go with the flow about doing Snapchat advertising and marketing and advertising and advertising and advertising and using it to assemble a following, promote your brand and pressure income?

The key to Snapchat is to recognize that it have to be part of a broader technique. That is to say which you're going to need to sell your self on extraordinary channels as properly earlier than you may begin diverting human beings to Snapchat.

And basically this may artwork through developing your goal marketplace on the ones channels – collectively with Facebook or Twitter – and then sharing your Snapchat to the ones channels. So as an example, you could create a video and then percentage it to Twitter and Instagram, further to saving it as your tale and sending it on your friends (we'll speak approximately the way to do this later).

This then we must folks who are following you on Facebook and on Twitter see what you're posting on Snapchat and the concept there can be of route that they'll assume it seems thrilling and therefore want to have a take a look at you. You really need to feature the video (we'll take a look at a way to do this later) after which upload the statement 'Add me on Snapchat for added of my adventures'… for exok.

Someone who does this very well within the suggest time is Arnold Schwarzenegger. Arnold is a person who has actually grasped the idea of social media and who is the use of it in very clever strategies to assemble a bigger audience and to

advantage new fans and followers. He has a big Facebook internet internet web page, Instagram ac

do not forget and extra – but possibly the channel he promotes most usually is his Instagram.

Recently, Arnie posts a photo of himself biking in a state-of-the-art city and stated that he in no way widely wide-spread the excuse that people 'don't have time to workout'. He accompanied this through manner of manner of saying he is going for a bike ride because the first detail he does on every occasion he receives to a modern-day metropolis and that he stocks that journey collectively together with his Snapchat fans.

Other instances, he's going to put up movement photos of himself talking at occasions, assembly different famous people and generally absolutely doing exciting matters that his enthusiasts may want to appearance. They then get updated collectively together together with his exploits and experience like they're getting nearly privileged get admission to to his way of lifestyles and sports. Every now after which he stocks those films on Facebook and so his fans see that in the event that they want to get extra specific and personal content material, they need to get onto Snapchat. For the ones expert internet marketers analyzing this, you'll apprehend that this is basically a earnings funnel and people humans now following him may be even greater dependable to the brand.

Remember: it takes 'five touches' to sell someone a few issue. So if you have visible a person on TV > favored them on Facebook > started out out following them on Snapchat... then you definately definately're already 3 touches in!

Facebook is one way to try this but there are various one of a kind social media channels which might be especially nicely appropriate to promoting Snapchat. Instagram is one extraordinary instance because it already allows you to percent short movies. Another acceptable desire for the same purpose is Vine.

Other Methods and Techniques for Building Viewers

There are of route different strategies you may collect a larger aim marketplace too. One instance is to certainly sell your self for your very personal weblog or internet website. This is absolutely how electronic mail marketing often works – with marketers selling their mailing list on their blogs and regularly which encompass an decide-in form right with every placed up, or otherwise in one of the sidebars.

Likewise, you could increase or promote your Snapchat thru a few different channel. A accurate instance is YouTube – actually state on the quit of your movies which you have a Snapchat channel wherein you located up greater one-of-a-type content material fabric material on your biggest lovers and try to make it sound exciting!

Another tool that you may use and that is famous in all styles of advertising and advertising and advertising, is influencer marketing and advertising. This in truth technique that you're teaming up with other influencers and sharing your purpose market. For example, you would possibly make a short video with each other outstanding persona on Snapchat after which mention the channel of that man or woman in your non-public video. Likewise, they may do the identical for you, letting you seem in a single in every of their films/snap shots and seasonedmoting your account within the method.

To make this artwork, you want to ensure which you method creators who're on the equal level as you and in the same area of interest. In unique words, when you have a health channel and also you promote fitness clothing, then you definately definately want to ensure which you work with distinctive health personalities on Snapchat – in any other case their lovers obtained't be inquisitive about following you! Likewise, you need to keep away from coming near the most critical names inside the business enterprise (like Arnie) due to the reality they get tens of hundreds and thousands of messages a day and gained't be probably to reply in your requests.

If you've got 2,000 fans, then technique a person else with 2,000 followers. Then, while you've done that some times and you've got 5,000 followers, you could start drawing close people with five,000 lovers! Think of it like a ladder and try to head closer to the pinnacle one rung at a time.

Monetizing

Finally, you get to monetize your channel or truely use it to reinforce your emblem. You've built the audience however in assessment to, say Pinterest, there is no shop built into Snapchat. What's the issue of building this form of large following?

Well, in the case of someone like Arnie, the surrender cease give up end result is clearly to enhance the emblem. If Arnold can get humans to conform along with his each day exploits on Snapchat and notice his updates from backstage, then the ones identical fans can be more likely to move and notice his new films at the same time as they arrive out in theaters. They will enjoy like larger fans, genuinely as a derivative of following him.

The identical can come up with the consequences you want when you have a blog, a YouTube channel or every other shape of channel which you need to promote in case you want to generate sales. This also can be a wonderful way to assemble agree with and authority, to set up yourself as a main professional on your given niche in order that human beings may be extra likely to be aware of you while you propose a product or try and sell your services.

And in the long run, you may of course use a Snapchat video or photograph to sell topics without delay. A correct way to do that for example is probably with a examine, in which

you may evaluate a product and then percentage the link in which your target market can circulate and buy it need to they be interested.

And because you have were given a 90% open rate and you're talking with them in a very direct way, with all the benefits of video... you can get a few pretty astounding conversion fees and strain a whole lot of profits this way.

In quick, it's miles very an lousy lot nicely worth a while installing that initial paintings up the the front that lets in you to get humans to observe you and to be

Chapter 35: Finding Your Way Around Snapchat's Basic Features

Now you recognize the basics of tactics you need to be the usage of Snapchat, the subsequent question is the way you pass about honestly placing that into motion. What does it bodily consist of in order with the intention to submit those films, percentage them on different channels and expand your intention market?

Getting Set Up

The first factor you'll want to do is to download Snapchat as an app for either the iPhone or Android. There is alas no laptop version of Snapchat and no website that does the identical element, consequently the most effective manner to apply it's far thru the use of the app.

Once you have the app in your tool, the subsequent element you need to do is to log in or be part of up. The new Snapchat has a quite polished and tremendous looking advent now, which functions a definite white interface along with your silhouette in the history, picked up through the virtual camera.

Signing up is short and painless. You may want to probably need to kind in a cellphone number, but Snapchat acquired't percent this with different clients. You can also be requested to skip a verification device concerning asking a query. On the following show, you'll have the selection to 'Find Friends', this isn't always uncommon with many apps of this nature. You can find out pals the use of numbers in your cope with e-book and it's a first-rate concept to characteristic the humans you realize – they can be your first lovers!

One you've done this, faucet the ghost photograph at the pinnacle of the display. This will will permit you to upload greater buddies and additionally 'tap to characteristic a selfie'. This is effectively your profile photograph and works just like a profile image on any other social net web page...

...Except that it's lively. A word of warning, at the same time as you hit the button, you'll have a short countdown and then a few separate snap shots may be taken on the way to be mixed to shape a short animation. Make fine you understand what you want to be doing in that animation in advance than it gets made! Once taken, you can then proportion this picture via Whatsapp or Facebook, which

might be an extraordinary manner to inform the arena you're beginning your Snapchat marketing!

This net web page additionally lets in you to function buddies if you want to, because of this you can find out those who aren't to your deal with ebook via manner of looking for them through their username. Try searching out ArnoldSchnitzel to comply with Arnie.

If you hit the cog button inside the top right inside the meantime, you'll be taken to the additional settings in which you may installation greater statistics approximately your account. This lets you edit your password, input your DoB and pick sure privateness options together with who can view your story and who can contact you. You also can find out the privateness coverage here, the terms of company and greater.

One very crucial exchange to make proper right here is who can view your story. You need to trade this from 'My Friends' to 'Everyone' and that allows you to make sure that folks that follow you could see your story, not honestly the people you're following over again!

Sending Snaps

Once you've lengthy gone via this approach, you'll now be capable of begin the use of Snapchat right away!

The most important display is basically similar to your digital digital digicam – you'll simply see what your digicam lens sees but with some buttons overlaid on top. While the device is pretty smooth when you get the hold of it, the UX is in reality no longer that intuitive and hundreds of people will use Snapchat for a long time without ever uncovering all of the competencies! That's in which this e-book is available in very on hand for marketers hoping to get the very maximum out of it.

To supply a snap, all you need to do is to take a photograph thru tapping the big round button within the bottom middle of the display. This will then take you to a preview of that picture and also you currently have a few unique alternatives.

In the bottom left, you have got a photo of a clock. This icon allows you to set the period of your image which can be one to ten seconds. This defines how lengthy your recipients can view the photograph for earlier than it disappears. Note although that there are numerous strategies they could beat back this predicament inside the occasion that they need to – no longer least by using method of actually taking a display seize if they have an Android tool!

Next to that icon is a downward pointing arrow. This is actually the 'download' alternative and will shop the photograph you've truely taken in your cellphone. This may be very available because it manner you could now percent it some other place, which as we've stated is one of the crucial methods you could broaden your following.

Next to that could be a square with a plus within the corner. This essentially technique you are together with the image for your 'story'. Essentially, your 'tale' is an internet net page wherein your follower is probably able to see all your photographs and pics from the closing 24 hours in collection. This is a great manner to allow human beings seize up with content you've created in a extra traditional way.

In the top left, you've got were given a pencil icon. This permits you to draw for your image the use of your finger. If you have got a

Samsung Galaxy Note device, then you could provoke people with some extra unique sketches. You'll be able to select the shade of your scrawls via using clicking on the colored squares that drop down from the left by the use of that icon.

Next to that is a 'T' icon. This lets in you to feature annotations to your photo and textual content, which can be extraordinary for funny captions or messages.

Then there are the stickers. Hit the square on the pinnacle left this is slightly askew and this could supply up a menu of stickers. These consist of numerous popular acronyms and examples of textspeek, speech bubbles, pictures of rabbits and animals and all manner of various topics. Once determined on, you can then drag them all through the show show screen with your finger. Think of those a chunk like emojiis. You also can pick the elegance of sticker to leap without delay to them via the usage of the icons down the lowest.

One final element you can do is to swipe left. Doing this may supply up some of filters further to a few greater artwork which will alternate frequently to be topical. This is also based on place and time data taken from your smartphone, for instance you can add the time (inside the shape of a digital clock) or you can add photographs applicable to in that you're located. I'm positioned in Lon

don and proper now there are alternatives to percent snap shots of London. Likewise, I may have frames which is probably concerning the EU debate within the UK, because of the reality the vote on that is first-rate multiple days away. There's moreover the selection to feature greater traditional filters, which includes a black and white preference or a blue one in case you need to make your photo appear like current paintings. Just keep swiping left to scroll thru your options.

Finally, whilst you're completed editing, you could then hit the send button (the blue arrow) and then pick out who you want to send your tale to out of your friends list.

When you create your snap, you need to pick to ship it on your tale, or you can try this thru the use of the picture button. This is critical, as it's miles how you could deliver your story proper away to your fans so that everybody can see it.

Of course you may always add absolutely one in every of your lovers again after which begin to ship them person snaps and movies. This way, you could supply them focused content material to try and promote to them and that could be a very advanced, albeit powerful, way to market your self.

For maximum human beings even though, the nice approach is in reality to characteristic movement pics for your tale and then allow them to see while you replace that!

www.ingramcontent.com/pod-product-compliance
Lightning Source LLC
Chambersburg PA
CBHW071222210326
41597CB00016B/1915